Resurrecting Your Hope

Reignite the Hope You've Lost

Shelly Skiver

<u>**Disclaimer**</u>
Every effort has been made to format this book so that you have a good experience reading it. Despite these efforts, however, sometimes formatting problems may occur through the conversion process. Should formatting problems occur through your download of this publication as an e-book or when it is converted to paperback, the author Shelly Skiver and her representatives and agents, are not responsible for this. Unfortunately, no refund for formatting problems will be available.

The concepts and suggestions in this book are suggestions only. While it is the hope and intention of Ms. Skiver, and her representatives and agents, that only positive life improvements result from reading and applying the concepts within, any negative consequences of life decisions made by the reader are not the responsibility of the author.

"Hope deferred makes the heart sick
But a longing fulfilled is a tree of life."
Proverbs 13:12

"Resurrecting Your Hope"
is dedicated to my beautiful children,
Christopher and Faith.
In looking at you each day,
my hope for the future is renewed.
This book is also dedicated to you; the reader.
It is *my* hope that this book
helps *your* hope be resurrected,
and that you will be set upon
your "God-Track."

Table of Contents

It had all but dried up,
the substance of my veins.
But when my eye looked up,
lo and behold…I dazed…
yet a tiny spark remains.

-Shelly Skiver

1

How to Get the Most
Out of This Book

Hope, by definition, means: to expect with confidence; trust. It is the forward-looking mental attitude of having the reasonable expectation that what you want to happen, will happen. To have hope means that you believe everything will work out for the best.

In order to look forward with trust and confidence that everything will be good…or at least alright…you need a past that has conditioned you to believe that. It's difficult to feel good about your future unless something good has happened in your past….something good you can draw from. Many people today have hardships and difficulties lasting so long that they've become conditioned to expect more of the same going forward…more disappointment, more heartache…and that has led them to feel hopeless.

Is that how you've been feeling about *your* future?

If so, you are not alone. Lately, this world has been a difficult place in which to live, and for many people, hope has been hard to find.

That was true for my family members and me. For too many years we experienced one loss after another; set-backs, accidents, financial blight, diseases and deaths. Just when I thought I could take no more, another tragedy would hit, and on and on it went until the only word that could describe us was "longsuffering." Eventually, I became conditioned to expect the worst, not the best. I gave up the hope that my future would be any good and came to believe that only tragedy, poverty, and ensuing death were my fate. Hope had become nothing to me but an elusive, flitting butterfly that had regressed back into its slimy, larval bug stage, then crawled under a rock somewhere in a far and distant land. My heart had grown cold and hard, and I was pretty sure *hope* would be impossible to find, ever again.

Proverbs 13:12 says, *"Hope deferred makes the heart sick, but a longing fulfilled is a tree of life."*

My heart was, indeed, sick for too long. But then, as my life finally began to get healed and somewhat stabilized (a necessary condition for healing to take place), my hope began to come back to life. That, in and of itself, is a miracle. Hope resurrected. That's what many people need, and they need it now.

Hope is life-giving entity. It is a crucial quality-of-life factor that is unmatched in value and importance. With hope life springs forth again with vitality, energy, joy, and a confidence that you're about to live out good things. Hope is the only life-giving force that can pull people up from the mire.

On the contrary, without hope there is *no* life; nothing to look forward *to*. If all hope becomes lost…even hope for a better *distant* future…the futility of this condition may become fatal. The statistics on suicide prove this instantly. The World Health Organization states that 1 Million people commit suicide each year. And that's only the number that "succeed" out of all those who try - which is a staggering 20 Million. I have two close friends whose sons became so hopeless for so long, they both attempted suicide; one was successful; one was not. I'll recount one of their miraculous stories in Chapter 14.

Hopeless thoughts can ask questions like this: "What good is my future if it's not going to be any better than my past?" or "What good is my future if I can't fix the mistakes of my past?" Hope answers: "Although the past brought bad things - be it grief, fear, tragedy, or despair - your future does not have to be like the past, no matter how long those bad things have been going on."

"But," you say, "I hoped and hoped that things would change, and change never came. Things stayed the same for so long, I finally gave up. Why hope for things to change when they never do?" Hope answers: "Even when hope is deferred again and again, as long as you have breath, there is hope for a brighter future, but only if you don't give up. Giving up; that's the only *real* hopeless state to be in."

In this book, I'll give you some tools to help you restore your hope, so that, even if you've given up on hope entirely, you will experience a "Hope Resurrection" and you'll walk away with a renewed sense of hopefulness for your future.

The main ingredient to resurrecting your hope is God. God *is* the God of hope. To reject God is to reject hope; to reject life. What good could possibly come of walking down that track? Even in the face of catastrophe, God provides hope to the hopeless.

"Blessed are those whose help is the God of Jacob, whose hope is in the LORD their God."
Psalm 146:5

"May the God of hope fill you with all joy and peace as you trust in him, so that you may overflow with hope by the power of the Holy Spirit."
Romans 15:13

If you have become so disheartened that you've turned away from God, I urge you to reconsider that decision. With God there's always hope and without Him there is none. Scripture is very clear on this and there are multitudes of people who can attest to it. With God and prayer, you *will* see many miracles.

I will cite many scriptures as we refocus our perspective on God; some of the same verses repeatedly. I'll do more than just that, though…more than just focusing on God in a general way. This book will give you simple steps you can take to find what purpose God has for your life. Doing this is tantamount to having…and keeping…hope for yourself. To unlock the door of hope, and to keep that door open once and for all in your life, I believe you must find your God-mandated purpose, or your "God-Track." *You* have one, and I am convinced that as we get closer and closer to the return of Jesus, He needs you to find and fulfill your earthly mission more now than ever before in your life. As long as you have breath, your work on earth is not done. In fact, you are more important now than ever before in history. You are needed and it may be that you're about to be "called up" for active duty.

In fact, finding and fulfilling your God-Track is so important for "such a time as this," that it's possible that the Lord has been blighting the path you've been on, if it's not the "right" one. This was the case in my own life. My self-sufficient path…seeking my own agenda for my life…was the only path I knew, so I fervently pursued it. I believed that I was to be a successful business professional, but God had something else in mind. As I kept chasing down the path of my own plan, God kept blighting that path, causing me years of frustration, confusion and despair. Only when my circumstances were completely desperate did I seek Him and listened to Him; then He showed me what it was that He wanted me to do. As shocked as I was, He made it very clear to me, so I began to pursue *His* path for my life. Over the process of time, after a period of trial and preparation had been completed, my hope began to resurrect as I rose to fulfill my God-Track. God needed my cooperation in order to accomplish the things that He created and planned for me to do. When I cooperated with Him and His time of refining was completed, my "life-blight" began to be healed, bringing hope back into my life.

In "Resurrecting Your Hope," I'll show you the simple steps the Lord took me through to find my God-Track, so I could become maximally useful to Him. You can apply them to your own life, too, and the light of hope will shine on you, once again.

By the time you finish this book you should be able to fill in the blanks below:

Your mission, _____,
               (your name here)

should you decide to accept it, is:

_____

_____

_____

Fulfilling this mandate for your life – your God-Track - will give you an *unbreakable* hope for your future. Your future is bright on your God-Track because that's the only place where God's mercy, favor, prosperity and fruitfulness are. This is what you need in order to have real quality of life: Hope rooted in purpose.

There are other reasons that lead to hopelessness besides not being on your God-Track. Some people have been victims of heinous abuse or other violent crimes. Some have lived through natural disasters, calamities, or have experienced other life tragedies. Know that God is the God Who redeems your life from the pit, and Who crowns you with love and compassion (Psalm 103). With God all things are possible (Mark 9:23; Matthew 19:26); there is always a reason to have, at least, a smidgeon of hope. There's nowhere on earth that God can't reach. Please keep reading and don't give up.

"You answer us with awesome and righteous deeds, God our Savior, the hope of all the ends of the earth and of the farthest seas..."
Psalm 65:5

Also, please know that I am praying for you. While this book was formulating in my mind, I was praying for you; as I was writing it, I was praying for you. I hope that God will accomplish in you and through you, all that He intends. Let Him.

2

Using Haggai

Haggai 2:4-5

"'But now be strong, Zerubbabel,' declares the LORD. 'Be strong, Joshua son of Jozadak, the high priest. Be strong, all you people of the land,' declares the LORD, 'and work. For I am with you,' declares the LORD Almighty. 5 'This is what I covenanted with you when you came out of Egypt. And my Spirit remains among you. Do not fear.'"

Throughout "Resurrecting Your Hope," I will place scripture references in the text that will provide an example of what God says in the matter, or that will illustrate the point of discussion. I'll often use scripture from the book of Haggai. In fact, the verses above are intentionally stated repeatedly throughout "Resurrecting Your Hope."

Haggai was a prophet through whom God spoke to a people who were completely forlorn, providing them with specific promises about their future, *if* they would get on their God-mandated God-Track. Like me, these ancient Israelites had not been fulfilling their God-Track, and therefore their lives had been blighted in every way. Haggai has within it the keys you need to unlock the door that leads to the path of hope itself; promises of restoration and a life filled with purpose. After Haggai spoke and the Israelites got on their God-Track, they ended up experiencing a complete turnaround of their lives.

On the surface, God was addressing the financial blight the Israelites had been experiencing, but the book of Haggai is about so much more than just finances. Using Haggai, God spoke to His people about the condition of blight that was affecting *every area* of their lives. That blighted condition of the ancient Jews' lives was something I've experienced as well. I've come to refer to it as "life-blight." *Everything* in their lives was failing to thrive – their physical health; their safety as a people group; their homes; their relationships; their finances, crops, cattle and livestock; and even their outlook toward a better future. Yes, even their hope was blighted. They were spiritually blighted; they lacked a commitment to God and His purposes as their number one priority; and it showed.

It showed in the most important of all ways. The Jews returning to Jerusalem out of Babylon had set aside the rebuild project of the ruined temple – that was the entire purpose for which God had brought them out of Babylon and restored them to their homeland, in the first place. God's temple was sitting there in ruins right before their eyes, and they had been ignoring it. In fact, as it turned out, that was the *whole* problem.

Since the day those Jews…aka the "Returning Remnant"…had come out of captivity in Babylon and returned to their homeland some eighteen years prior, a lot had happened to them. They'd had a rough road. Imagine the high hopes they'd had upon being released out of captivity. Finally, they were being set free from almost fifty years of subjection to their enemies and allowed to return to their beloved homeland! However, instead of the peace and prosperity they'd expected, they were met with violent enemy attacks which eventually led them to stop their

18

God-mandated purpose; the building God's temple. But their fear only made their situation worse. When they decided to stop building the temple and turned their focus to material gain, God was displeased with them. Accidents, financial destitution and poverty, death and disease, followed. While they pursued financial gain as their top priority, God had imposed upon them what could only be defined as a curse. He did this to get them back to what *He* had ordained for them to do. He cursed one path and blessed another, according to Haggai's words.

While on the wrong track, those poor Jews must have been overwhelmingly confused and frustrated. However, we can benefit from their experiences and what God said to them about it. If we extract some of the principals from these and other scriptures, including God's promises to them for a brighter future, we can apply them to ourselves in order to bring clarity to the confusion. Using Haggai, we can bring better understanding to what God has been doing in our own lives.

My hope is that you will then find out what God's purpose is for your life...then can you get on your God-Track...the only path for you that's blessed by God. That is where He wants you to be.

Maybe you've held onto a dream for years, even decades, and worked very hard to achieve that dream. Yet, all of your efforts; all of your investments; all your hard work toward the goal you've held up in your life didn't pan out, leaving you with nothing but a bleak outlook.

Or, maybe your hope has faded, or even died, due to something else; you may have been a victim of something atrocious that occurred in this world. What could God possibly say was the reason for that pain? How can you ever move past that trauma; just doing what others say to do - "get over it" and move on with your life? That may seem impossible from your current vantage point. Your heart may feel like it's broken into so many pieces that it would be impossible to fix, but I assure you, it can be, and you can be better than you ever were.

We'll look for reasons for your pain and suffering, but in some instances, we won't find an explanation because maybe God hasn't yet revealed to you what He's doing in your life. God may be delaying your answer, as He did for many years in my own life. I did not know, and couldn't understand, why God was blighting everything I touched. When I asked Him, He wouldn't tell me. Until one day He finally did.

When we don't find the answers we seek, we'll look for faith, because faith kicks in when reason and logic leave us hanging without answers. And that's just the way it is. There may seem to be no explicable reason on earth for what's happened to you.

One automatic explanation for the terrible things that happen here is the fact that this is a fallen world and it is not our home. This world *is* perishing, the Bible says. In fact, the Bible explains many of the things that are happening on the earth today. Jesus told us that evil would increase, especially toward the end of the Church Age, causing the love of many, for God and for others, to grow cold. These words of Jesus describe the times we're living in *right now*. The main goal you want for your life is that you never let these words describe *you*. Do not let your love for God grow cold; if you do, the devil wins; all of the bad things that happened to you, win. Do not let that be your fate.

It may be that God has withheld promises He has made to you in the past, because He's been refining your faith, or because He's proud of you for how you've held up under immense pressure. He may be developing your character or preparing you for your destiny. It may be that God is going to call you to do a myriad of things that only you can do. This book is filled with examples of people just like you – people who felt abandoned by

God and as though the world had abused them terribly - but their stories will inspire you and help your hope to be resurrected.

There are many reasons to still have hope for your life. Even in the darkest hour, when it seems that all is lost, God still has His hand on you. When you can't feel His presence and have no visible sign that He remembers you, I assure you - He does.

"But God will never forget the needy; the hope of the afflicted will never perish."
Psalm 9:18

Through the prophet Haggai, God told the people, *"Give careful thought to your ways."* In fact, God said this particular phrase five times in this short book of only 38 total verses. Why did God keep telling the suffering, downtrodden people to give their ways careful thought? They didn't have the energy to meditate thoughtfully on anything; you've never seen a more disheartened people. However, it was important for God to get the people to realize that He wanted them to carefully ponder what He was telling them. It was as though God was standing before them, shaking them by their shoulders saying, "Pay attention to Me. Think about what I am telling you now."

You may not have much energy right now to give careful thought to anything, either. That's the purpose of this book. It will give you easy steps and hopefully act as your bridge to a lighter, brighter life with God, fulfilling your purpose. Don't give up yet. At the end of each chapter I'll give you something specific about which to "Give Careful Thought." Something to ponder, with whatever time and energy you can give to it. Try to think about *it* instead of the reasons you are lacking in hope right now. There may also be a suggested prayer to pray in the "Give Careful Thought" section. Write in this book, take notes, and write down your thoughts. Let this book become your guide to a renewed outlook on your life.

If this world, the behavior of others, a tragedy, a series of tragedies, or other traumatic circumstances have caused you to feel like your hope has been trampled on until nothing is left but dead stubble, you should know…there is still cause for hope, even if you can't see it or feel it right now. Your hope, which I believe is vital to your life, *can* be resurrected. First, you must realize that I can't do it for you; and you can't even do it for yourself. However, there is One Who can redeem anything and everything in this world. He'll just need a little of your participation. If you don't have anything left to give, don't worry; just be *willing* to let Jesus heal and resurrect your hope. That's all you really need in order for Jesus to do something extraordinary for you. Just be willing to let Him.

In the back of this book is a list of God's Attributes. I added this list into the book because, when you focus more on the stunning attributes of God and His character, instead of your own circumstances, your hope can't help but be elevated.

Give Careful Thought:
Suggested Prayer:
"Lord, I will be willing to let You resurrect my hope, even though I have little faith that that's possible right now. Just like the man in Mark 9: 22-24 asked Jesus to help him with his unbelief, please help me with *my* unbelief! Where I lack trust in You, please help me to trust. Where I lack faith in You or in Your goodness, please help me with my unbelief. Wherever I have an inaccurate view of You, please help me. I'm willing to let Your Holy Spirit and Your Words mold my perception and my path to what You would have them be. Thank You, Lord. Amen."

Look up and write out Mark 9:22-24 below:
Mark 9:22-24:

3

Hope to God

Acts 17:28
*"For in Him we live and move
and have our being."*

Psalm 139:13
*"For You created my inmost being;
You knit me together
In my mother's womb."*

Psalm 9:18
*"But God will never forget the needy;
the hope of the afflicted will never perish."*

You were created by God and He doesn't do anything by happenstance or without meaning. You weren't an accident; you were created with painstaking care and meticulous attention to detail. Cell by cell you were put together. Your life has tremendous value, significance, and a specific purpose, even if you can't see it right now. Or, even if your future hope has been clouded by the fog of unanswered prayers and suffering from your past; even longsuffering. You may have endured difficult circumstances which lasted longer than you ever thought you could endure. Don't give up. Your hope for a better life is much closer and more accessible than you may think. You're almost there...just keep on praying and putting one foot in front of the other...as you read this book and "give careful thought" to each short chapter. Let God do the heavy lifting to restore your soul. He is the only One Who can do such a thing – no man and no book has that kind of power.

You may have asked God to help you with something repeatedly, but that help seemingly never came. You've given up. You've asked and asked and....nothing has formulated yet; nothing has changed yet. Each time you put your hope and faith in the Lord to change things for the better, your hopes were dashed. You're not alone; this has happened to many people I've spoken with. In fact, this happened to my family members and to me.

The ancient Returning Remnant were in a similar situation. In fact, they had grown so disheartened that they became paralyzed. First, they were paralyzed with fear. Then, out of their fear they changed course and veered into a whole different direction. They changed their priorities and decided it would be a good idea to focus on making money instead of rebuilding God's temple. However, on this new course, they weren't fulfilling their God-Track. Over time, their hopes for a prosperous life in their beloved homeland with their new-found freedom had been replaced with only scourge, and it affected the entire population. They had expected much, but received little. And God knew exactly what was in their hearts:

"Now this is what the LORD Almighty says: "Give careful thought to your ways. 6 You have planted much, but harvested little. You eat, but never have enough. You drink, but never have your fill. You put on clothes, but are not warm. You earn wages, only to put them in a purse with holes in it."
9 "You expected much, but see, it turned out to be little."
Haggai 1:5-6, 9

The Israelites couldn't understand why God, Who they knew was omnipotent and sovereign, had let all those bad things happen to them. Their faith had taken a severe beating. Their enemies had been successful in stopping them from rebuilding their lives, their homes, and more importantly, God's Temple. They had become completely ineffectual. They were without purpose and without hope, but God was doing something; something important to Him and something that would affect generations to come. Sometimes, when you can't see the reasons for the blight you've been experiencing, it's because God is doing something important in and through your life. While you're going through it - before God reveals what it is – that is a crucial period because it's a time of preparation and testing. It can also be, and usually is, a time of immense frustration and stress. I urge you to grab ahold of God now and hold onto Him. He has a hope and a future for you, and it can only be found in Him.

Be willing to give God license to restore your hope as only He can do and to show you what His purposes are for you.

Give Careful Thought:
If you suffer from a diminished sense of hope, in any way, I want you to open your heart to the idea of allowing God into your life. If you are in a desperate condition, or in despair, please pray this prayer:
"Lord Jesus, I pray right now that You will come into my soul and give me a new Spirit and a new understanding. May You live in me from this day forward, Lord. Restore my hope. I need something to hold onto after having my hope deferred for so long. I know that only You can restore my soul; that You are that Tree of Life I need. You are my only hope for finding my true purpose and fulfilling my longing. Please come with Your healing and

resurrecting power and renew my strength like the eagle's. Thank You, Jesus. Amen."

Meditate on these Scriptures:

Romans 15:5-6
"May the God who gives endurance and encouragement give you the same attitude of mind toward each other that Christ Jesus had, so that with one mind and one voice you may glorify the God and Father of our Lord Jesus Christ."

Jeremiah 29:11
"For I know the plans I have for you," declares the LORD, "plans to prosper you and not to harm you, plans to give you hope and a future."

Haggai 2:18
"...From this day on I will bless you."

Lord, let that day be today.

4

Ray of Hope

A few months before my dad died, my sister, Sue, went to visit him at his house. At the time, she was going through one of the hardest seasons of her life. Her marriage of twenty years was breaking apart; she and her husband were selling their home, so Sue was packing up to move. Her tumultuous situation was made worse as our dad's health declined.

As Sue was driving along, she was full of anguish and despair; crying, almost uncontrollably. She called out to the Lord, "I really need you to show me something good, *please, Lord*! I just need some kind of a ray of hope that you're there, and everything's going to be okay. Please just give me anything…any *ray of hope*, Lord, that's all I ask!" She arrived at my dad's, and visited with him for the afternoon until he wanted to lie down to rest. Then she left and headed home.

Our dad lived way out in the country, so when she left, Sue trucked her way down the dirt roads to the highway nearest his house – the route she always took home. Her heart was still full of despair because she knew our dad's health was not good…he was going downhill and things looked so bleak…and so, as she drove along, she was still asking God for some sort of a ray of hope – anything good to help her out of her hopeless pit. When she got to the highway, she had to turn left. An SUV was approaching from the right, so she waited for it to pass. When it did, she pulled out making her left turn onto the highway, behind the SUV. As she sped up and came up behind that vehicle, she was astounded to realize that the license plate on it was personalized. It read:

RAYHOPE

Sue knew immediately that God had answered her prayer, telling her by way of Divine Synchronicity, which could've never been achieved by any man, that Jesus was with her, that He had heard her prayer, and He was now giving her a message: there *was* a reason to have a "Ray of Hope"…and that reason was *Him*. No one will ever be able to convince me – not in a million years – that that was a coincidence. No human being could have made up those circumstances, caused them to be timed so perfectly, and then brought them all together for that to occur. It would be impossible….*impossible.*

Give Careful Thought:
Have you ever had a "Ray of Hope" moment like the one my sister, Sue, had? Do you keep a journal of prayers and answers to prayer? (If you haven't gotten into the habit of journaling regularly, I recommend that you start right away.) Think back to a time when something good happened as a result of a cry of your heart. Savor the memory of that answer to prayer and remember – God is the God of Hope. He accomplishes the impossible,

performing miracles on your behalf. And He is steadfast and unchanging; if He did it before, He will do it again.

Matthew 19:26
"Jesus looked at them and said, 'With man this is impossible, but with God all things are possible.'"

Suggested Prayer:
Lord Jesus, I believe that You can fulfill my longing and perform miracles in my life. Please do the impossible for me. Please hear the cry of my heart from Your throne in heaven and please help me in my life. Please act on my behalf. Amen.

5

The Rollercoaster of Chronic Hurt

When my family members and I went through years of tragedies, I wasn't prepared for it. I doubt you can get prepared for longsuffering (my *least favorite* word in this world).

When you're living at a certain baseline, even if it's at a much lower level than you expected for your life, at least you have the stability of that baseline. Sometimes maintaining that lower level of living can be better than the ups and downs associated with elevating your hopes, then repeatedly having them fall down. The baseline that you once had becomes something to covet because, at least, it was stable. Hopefulness causes your emotions to rise, but once you realize that the thing you'd hoped for isn't going to happen, the disappointment of that causes our emotions to dive to a level below where we were in the first place – back at that former baseline.

I often wished that I had never gotten my hopes up in the first place, because each time they were let down it only hurt worse and worse.

Eventually I just became numb to hoping; numb to everything.

Hope involves risk. The act of hoping for something is, in and of itself, an act of risk because you're investing emotionally in the desired outcome. In fact, the amount of risk involved in what you're hoping for is exactly proportionate to the amount of emotional attachment you've placed on the outcome.

For example, if you hope the ice cream truck comes down your street today, the risk attached to that hope is minimal. If it never comes, your let-down is something you can live with. The emotional risk involved in your "hope investment" was low.

However, if you've hoped again and again for something very valuable – maybe a child, or that you'll be cured of a debilitating disease – these are "high risk" investments in hope because they carry with them strong emotional attachments. If that child or that cure doesn't come year after year, the heart can grow sick, just like the Bible says it will.

"Hope deferred makes the heart sick, but a longing fulfilled is a tree of life."
Proverbs 13:12

This happens to people who have suffered what psychologists call "moral injury." This term is used to describe the trauma often suffered by veterans, first responders, medical professionals, and others who have experienced high-stress, trauma-inducing environments. Those who are victims of violent crimes, such as rape or abuse, can also suffer from moral injury.

Most people care about other human beings; they care about the sanctity of life and hold to these values. They expect other people to behave in a way that is consistent with these core values and beliefs. If they're forced into a situation where they either become a part of, or bear witness to, things they recognize as morally hideous, their conscious minds are not capable of reconciling what they're seeing with their core values. The subconscious mind must take over in order to prevent further damage to the psyche. This can cause the "glazed-over" look that many trauma victims have in their eyes. My son had that look at

34

the age of six after being horribly emotionally abused by someone he should've been able to trust in his life. It was then that he was diagnosed with P.T.S.D. Most people know about P.T.S.D. (Post-Traumatic Stress Disorder) these days – or at least they think they do - because it's become a commonly-used term in our culture. However, until you, or a close loved one, actually live through the devastating effects of P.T.S.D., (which I hope you never have to do), you will never understand the deep wounds to the soul that have occurred in the victims of this disease.

When the circumstances of this world assail our very moral conscience, something is terribly wrong. Maybe this describes you. Maybe you've been through something that you know was so wrong that you think nothing can ever again make it right.

"Don't give up. You've come this far! You're almost there; keep going."

When I was a teenager, I was invited to go to East Africa for summer school. A local math teacher and her husband were chaperoning a group of students from my school for the trip. During that trip, some of us took a side excursion to climb Mt. Kilimanjaro. This experience turned out to be one of the hardest things I've ever done in my life; an experience in which I, finally…several days after starting upward…overcame agonizing challenges and achieved a big victory.

However, on the first day of the climb I experienced the pain of "rollercoaster syndrome." This day, much of the 11-mile hike was up and down rolling, grassy hills which inclined increasingly upward. These hills looked like they came out of the movie "The Sound of Music." They seemed perfectly innocent and beautiful. However, after hours of hiking up and down them, even the downward, far end of each hill became painful. In fact,

35

for me, going downhill became more difficult than going uphill. When I noticed this, I was perplexed by it. Logic told me that climbing uphill utilizes more strenuous muscle tension than going downhill, but in reality, it was the opposite. To go downhill, for what seemed like the ten-thousandth time, I had to exercise discipline while feeling exhausted. I had to fight the urge to just let go and roll down each hill; I had to fight against gravity. If I had obeyed the urge and just let go, I was afraid that I would fall down and roll, which held the potential risk of injury, and that could put my entire climb…even my life…in peril.

That's why I call the downside of hope "the far side of hope hill." On the way up the hill, you're hoping for something. Once you get to the pinnacle - or the top - it's decision time. The decision may not be yours to make, but here you'll discover if what you've been hoping for will or will not happen. If it isn't going to happen as you had hoped, you begin your "climb" down the far side of hope hill – in disappointment you may go lower than you were when you started hoping in the first place. This is why there is risk associated with hope.

Once I made it to the top of Mt. Kilimanjaro successfully, the immense challenge of achieving that victory became something that kept me going through longsuffering, later in my life. During the climb of Kibo peak…which was done during the middle of the night…I often thought of giving up. I couldn't see how I could keep climbing in the dark, bone-chilling cold. My nose was bleeding, my feet were in agonizing pain, I was fighting nausea, and struggling for every breath of thin air. But I had a "saving grace." Walking directly behind me in the single-file line, up that peak, was my friend, Leanne. Every time I talked about turning back she'd say to me, "Keep going, Shelly! You can do it. Don't turn back. You've come this far!" "But my nose won't stop bleeding, I'm going to throw up, and I can't breathe!" I'd whine to her. "Shelly, you've come this far. Don't give up. Keep going!"

Leanne would tell me again and again. She was instrumental in helping me make it to the summit of that mountain, several grueling hours later.

As the years passed, especially when things became extremely challenging for my family members and me, that climb became a metaphor for my life. When going through difficult cancer treatments, I thought about Leanne encouraging me. In my mind I could hear her voice telling me, "Keep going, Shelly! You've come this far; don't give up now!" When going through years of the chronic pain associated with spinal stenosis, I thought about Leanne and that climb, once again. I do credit her with the fact that I successfully made it to the summit of Mt. Kilimanjaro – a *huge* accomplished in itself. But I also credit Leanne and the success of that climb with helping me make it through cancer; spinal stenosis; the grief of losing both of my parents; losses of businesses as well as many more losses and challenges. As the difficult years marched on, I kept seeing Leanne's face and hearing her tell me, "Keep going, Shelly! You can do it; you've come this far; you're almost there!"

Are you tired of living; tired of the ups and downs of life, tired of being in a state of chronic pain? Have you longed for something that has never materialized in your life…to have a chronic disease healed or to have some financial stability, once and for all…only to have your hopes deferred time and time again? Of course, I can't tell you that I have the answer and that today's the day your longing will be realized. Only God knows that. But what I have learned, I will give to you.

The Bible says that Jesus wept over Jerusalem. It describes Jesus as a "man of sorrows and acquainted with grief." The Bible also says He took the burden of all sin – of the entire fallen world and all of its effects on humanity – to its death, along with Him, on the cross. As you read through the New Testament, especially the Gospels, you can't help but be inspired and amazed at all the miracles that Jesus performed. He never left *anyone* untouched; unhealed by Him. He resurrected people who had died and brought them back to life. Then, He lovingly and willingly took sin and death and put *them* to death on our behalf!

Don't let Jesus' sacrifice for you be made in vain. If you're reading this right now, it's no coincidence. God does not do things by accident or as an afterthought; especially not when it comes to you. You've come this far; don't give up. Grace, healing and resurrecting power are yours for your life through Jesus Christ. Your life has meaning and a purpose. Don't give up; have faith and keep going.

Give Careful Thought:

Do you have a "Leanne" in your life; someone who can help you conquer this mountain that you've been climbing? There is undoubtedly someone – a friend, a parent, a pastor – someone you trust, in whom you can confide and who will pray for you. Reach out and remember what I said at the beginning of this book: I am praying for you.

Whatever the challenge is that has, at times, brought you hopelessness and even despair, I pray right now in THE NAME THAT IS ABOVE ALL NAMES; THE NAME OF JESUS CHRIST, that your hope will be resurrected. May your outlook be raised up, never to get downtrodden again. Amen.

Read the following Scriptures and give them careful thought:

Galatians 6:9

"Let us not become weary in doing good, for at the proper time we will reap a harvest if we do not give up."

Revelation 3:7-11

"...These are the words of Him who is holy and true, who holds the key of David. What He opens no one can shut, and what He shuts no one can open. I know your deeds. See, I have placed before you an open door that no one can shut. I know that you have little strength, yet you have kept my word and have not denied my Name. I will make those who are of the synagogue of satan……I will make them come and fall down at your feet and acknowledge that I have loved you. Since you have kept my command to endure patiently, I will also keep you from the hour of trial that is going to come on the whole world to test the inhabitants of the earth.
I am coming soon."

6

Have You Been Hurt by the Church or Other Christians?

Years ago, before I became a Christian, I lived in San Francisco. I had professional success and a busy social life. My spiritual beliefs were deeply embedded in "New Age" thinking, in which I believed there were many paths to God and Jesus was just one of them. The old Doobie Brothers' song, "Jesus is just alright with me," sort of summed up the way I thought of Him. Many of my friends were gay, and I leaned about as far away from conservative, Biblical beliefs and values as you could get.

I attended a New-Age "church" with about fifty gay guys, led by a bi-sexual pastor and his gay partner. They had an "open" relationship and would date other people, both male and female. All of us agreed on one thing: we didn't like Christians very much. In fact, I had a very negative view of Christians in general, but especially conservative Christian leaders.

Back then, in the late eighties and early nineties, there were several Christian leaders who were caught doing unsavory things. "See," I told myself, "these people represent all Christians; they are nothing but a bunch of hypocrites."

However, every time I had a judgmental thought like that about a Christian, a different thought would immediately float across my mind, like a soft voice, and it would say, *"Judge Me not by the deeds of men."* When Jim Bakker was charged with crimes and the PTL Club was imploding, I thought, "Those Christians are all the same; despicable." But then I heard that voice say, *"Judge Me not by the deeds of men."*

When Jerry Falwell took over the PTL Club, then began having arguments with the Bakkers who had been ousted, I thought, "See, just like I've always thought – they're all hypocrites." Again, I immediately "heard" that voice speak into my mind, *"Judge Me not by the deeds of men."* When Jimmy Swaggert was caught with a prostitute, the same thing happened.

In fact, every time I had a negative thought about a Christian, be it my own judgmental thoughts about a specific Christian leader, or just Christians in general, that voice spoke those words to me again and again. *"Judge Me not by the deeds of men."*

Once I discovered that I was pregnant, I left my professional position, moved back to the Midwest, and began regularly attending a Bible-based church for the first time. Eventually, I came to a belief in the One and Only, True God – Jesus Christ of the Bible.

And I finally asked myself, "Who is constantly saying to me, *'Judge Me not by the deeds of men?'*" (I wasn't hearing an actual, audible voice but rather a consistent thought). After some time of attending a Christian church based on truth, I finally realized that Jesus Himself had been speaking those words into my mind – by that time, for years. He was telling me not to base my decision about *Him* on the behaviors of *people*. I was utterly astounded by this.

That voice – *His voice* - had helped me overcome my objections to Christians, and doing that helped lead me to a soul-saving faith. I finally realized that Jesus is God and man is not. I stopped evaluating and judging Jesus based on the behaviors of humans, as I began a relationship with Jesus Christ on the basis of Who He is, and nothing but that truth.

Several years later I found myself faced with the same challenge. As loving and supportive as my church family had become to me, they disappointed me in a big way, and, once again, I found myself judging other Christians.

After six years of attending my beloved church, the leadership split. "My" pastor, Pastor Jim, was suddenly leaving "my" church! I was shocked and abhorred at this news because Pastor Jim had taught the uncompromising truth of the Gospel from the pulpit, and he was a tremendous influence in leading me to a saving knowledge of the Truth. I thought of him as my spiritual father, so to speak.

What unfolded over the following weeks and months was very disturbing to me. The other members of the church leadership had wanted to push Pastor Jim out for some time, but I, as well as many others in the congregation, were unaware of this. There was dissension among them, and even though Pastor Jim was an upright man, the others wanted him out, so after a three-month sabbatical, or cooling off period, the decision became final. Pastor Jim was leaving this once-thriving church where the Holy Spirit had flowed so generously.

This made me angry at the other members who were in leadership there. From my perspective, they were persecuting my "father." Many people felt this way and the entire church split apart. The place where I had felt such a sense of loving family and community; the place where I couldn't wait to go every Sunday morning and Wednesday night – was falling apart. And then, it was gone.

There are a lot of people in this world who have been badly hurt, even devastated, by religion and the church. Look at the atrocities perpetrated by so many priests in the Catholic Church. This is completely unacceptable. And as I look at the actions of the Westboro Baptist "Church" who have picketed at funerals of fallen veterans, adding to the pain and anguish of their families and loved ones, I am horrified. I don't believe they have acted out of love for, or obedience to, Jesus.

However, the Lord says, *"Judge Me not by the deeds of men."* Jesus did not condone the divisiveness that occurs in so many churches or the actions of priests who have abused children. Never, ever, would He do that. In fact, the Bible tells us that it would be better for those people who have abused children if they would've never been born.

I remember once, when my emotions from multiple traumas were still raw, going to a small-group meeting through a church I occasionally attended. The conversation turned to trusting God and I made a comment that I later regretted deeply. I said something like, "Well, it's hard to trust God when so many bad things happen to you." Numerous "lectures" ensued from this body of 12 people. By vehemently trying to change my outlook instead of accepting the way I felt, they only made my pain worse. Much worse. It was a horrible experience. I left there and I never went back.

Those people would have done less harm and more good, if they had just listened to me with understanding in their hearts, prayed with me, and let God take over from there. However, by then I knew what Jesus had told me: they were mere followers of Him; they weren't *Him.*

Don't let the behaviors of others who are (or merely claim to be) Christians disappoint you so much that their actions become an obstacle between you and Jesus. We, as Christians, are following Him and doing our best to become more like Him, but we're *not Him.* We are each a work in progress and because we're fallen human beings and He is God, we fall short of Him in every way.

People sometimes ask me, "How do I have a relationship with Jesus? I mean, He's not here." I always tell them the same thing...

First: He *is* here...just ask Him to show you and He will. When He does, you'll have no doubt about it.

Second: To have a personal, direct relationship with Jesus that is seen through the purest lens, you must read the Bible. That's the best way to learn about Him and know Him because that's where He can be found. The Word of God is *alive*. The Holy Spirit uses God's Word to communicate with you. There's no other way to explain this - you have to experience it for yourself. Start reading the Bible from front to back, even if you've read it before. Stay in Scripture daily and you will be amazed...probably mind-blown...by what happens.

Third: Talk to Jesus. You don't need any particular script or Biblically correct prayer. Just talk to Him...and as is the case in any relationship, you must also listen.

In your personal relationship with the Lord, you will still have disappointments; times of discouragement, and maybe even times of anger toward Him. Therefore, seeing Him for Who He is Himself, is the only way you can have a true relationship with Him. The one and only True God...He is the One you will find in The Bible.

Mark 9:42

Causing to Stumble

"If anyone causes one of these little ones—those who believe in me—to stumble, it would be better for them if a large millstone were hung around their neck and they were thrown into the sea."

If you've been hurt by a Christian person, or the members or leadership of a church, don't judge Jesus negatively because of the dysfunctional behaviors of Christian people. As I said, I did this before I became a Christian; the actions of *Christians* gave me a generally poor view of the real Jesus Christ. Then, out of His gracious mercy, He called to me and said, *"Judge Me not by the deeds of men."*

Give Careful Thought:

Jesus says, *"Judge Me not by the deeds of men."* Ask yourself, "How have I allowed the hurtful actions of others, especially Christian people, affect my perspective of Jesus Christ, Himself? How can I change that inaccurate perspective and try to gain a more honest view of Jesus?"

Here's a hint: start reading the Bible. Also, if you don't already attend church regularly, you may want to begin attending a church where the Bible is taught and preached, so you can learn more about it and about Jesus Christ.

Pray this prayer:

Lord Jesus, please forgive me for allowing my negative view of Christians, of the Church, or of the behaviors of people to become a stumbling block to me, preventing me from having faith in You.

Please guide me into the truth about You; the truth about God.

7

Hot and Cold

In Chapter 3 of the Book of Revelation, Jesus scolded the church of Laodicea because they were neither cold nor hot; their attitude toward the Lord had morphed into a state of tepidity. Jesus said to them: *"15) I know your deeds, that you are neither cold nor hot. I wish you were either one or the other! 16) So, because you are lukewarm – neither hot nor cold – I am about to spit you out of my mouth. "* **(Rev. 3: 15-16)**

Jesus was referring to three different heart attitudes toward Him:

First: Being "hot" toward Jesus is the condition many are in when they first believe and their hearts are burning for the Lord. This is also known as "the honeymoon period" in a new Christian's walk with Jesus, and it has the same meaning as it does in a marriage. Both people are often burning with love and passion for one another because of the novelty of being in a newly-born, newly-committed relationship and all the hopes and dreams that come along with that. During this phase in a believer's life, the Holy Spirit is often pouring out His presence generously as well as performing many miracles for the newborn Christian in order to solidify their faith and trust in Him. Much like it does later in a marriage relationship, this period eventually ebbs.

Second: When Jesus spoke about being "cold" toward Him, I believe He was talking about a phase many believers go through which includes disappointments, frustrations, and tests of our faith. We don't like that. Therefore, many Christians become bewildered, frustrated, and even angry with the Lord. These feelings are real, and they're more common than you may think. However, I've found they're not much talked about in the church.

Don't judge a Christian harshly if they're in this phase in their relationship with the Lord; it can also happen to you! And if you're the one going through deep disappointments, maybe even causing you to feel disappointed in, or mad at Jesus, don't add to your negative feelings by letting others make you feel guilty about it. Don't think being angry with Jesus is blasphemous. Don't be ridiculous…just maintain your respect for Him as the Preeminent Creator and Ruler of the Universe. In fact, when you think of Him that way, isn't it harder to be mad at Him? That's why I placed the list of the "Attributes of God" in the back of this book for easy reference. Your period of anger and disappointment may be reduced if you focus on the excellent and astounding attributes of the Lord.

What we have to realize about being hot and cold-hearted at Jesus is that both of these heart attitudes actually stem from a condition of love.

When I was in high school I was close to our school's principal, Mr. Van Riper. I worked in his office every morning for first hour. Sometimes my dad would bring me in late because he owned his own business, worked on his own schedule, and, sometimes, that schedule meant that I got delivered ten minutes late to school. This would make me mad at my father. One day, after I had expressed my anger toward my dad for getting me to my post late, my friend and my "boss," Mr. Van Riper, said to me, "Well, if you didn't love him, you couldn't get mad at him."

As a teenager, this was one of the most profound things I'd ever heard, and I knew Mr. Van Riper was right.

The same is true in our relationship with Jesus. If you didn't love Him, you couldn't get mad at Him. What He wants to have with you is a personal relationship. Relationships include periodic times of disappointment, frustration, and even anger with the other person. You're sometimes going to feel these things about Jesus and He's sometimes going to feel these things about you. Being angry with God, sometimes, is normal and believe me, Jesus can handle it.

If you're angry with Him, don't try to hide it from Him; that will do you no good since He is the One Who searches hearts. Admit it and ask God, Who is Above All Reproach, for His help with this condition; be willing to let go of your anger and cold-heartedness toward Him and toward others, and be healed. Don't stay in this condition for a long period of time, letting it turn into bitterness. Anger is a defense-emotion and you may have adopted it to protect yourself from some underlying devastation…even unconsciously. Ultimately, it will not serve you the way you may think. After a while, anger will hurt you more than help you.

Third: What is worse than being "hot" or "cold" in Jesus' eyes is becoming "lukewarm" toward Him. Long-term, chronic disappointment, anger, or bitterness, can eventually lead to this "lukewarm" state. Such chronic negative emotions are not good for you or for your relationship with Jesus…nor are they good for your loved ones. Remember…you love them! Do what is best for all of you as well as for your relationship with the Lord and be willing to lose your anger.

Again, this chronic condition of anger and bitterness can lead to the worst heart condition there is, according to Jesus Himself – the state of being lukewarm toward Him. This is the state of deliberate indifference. In the following chapter we are going to examine in more depth this heart-posture and the dangers it possesses.

Jesus is fully aware of how you feel and the state of your relationship with Him. He is full of forgiveness, grace and mercy. He knows that you have been hurt repeatedly and that, at times, you've blamed Him for not stopping it. He knows others have unfairly come against you and He doesn't want you to continue to suffer from the things that have happened in this damaged world, anymore.

Isn't it time to let go of that disappointment, anger, or whatever it is that's caused your heart to be "cold?" If you don't know how, just ask Jesus for His help and He *will* heal it for you.

"Ask and it will be done for you."
John 15:7

Give Careful Thought:
If you've been cold - angry at God because He let you go through more than you ever thought you could bear, or because you've asked and asked for something but He's never done it for you - it's time to forgive and let go of that anger. Don't let yourself become "lukewarm;" indifferent toward Jesus.

Take a few minutes to review some of God's Attributes in the back of this book. Then ask Jesus to search your heart; to heal and to remove any anger or other form of "coldness" that you've had toward Him. Ask Him to stoke the fire in your heart for Him, and to make your heart burn for Him again.

8

Lukewarm

Revelation 3: 15-16
"I know your deeds, that you are neither cold nor hot. I wish you were either one or the other! So, because you are lukewarm – neither hot nor cold – I am about to spit you out of my mouth."

Jesus would prefer that you were on fire for Him. However, if you're not on fire, He would apparently prefer it if you were "cold" toward Him, rather than "lukewarm," according to His own words. Why does He hate it so much when someone becomes lukewarm toward Him? Why does He hate that so much, that He tells the Laodiceans that He's going to "spit them out of His mouth" because of the lukewarm condition of their hearts toward Him?

As we discussed in the last chapter, our heart attitudes of "hot" and "cold" indicate deep feelings toward Jesus. If we're hot or cold it means we're either "on fire" for the Lord (hot) or we're feeling mad, frustrated, or deeply disappointed (cold) toward Him. But even when we're cold toward Him, this still expresses a condition of love.

Being "lukewarm," though; that's the worst possible state to be in spiritually because it reveals that your love has died. There isn't anything left…you feel empty inside… maybe due to longsuffering or long-term hopelessness. Moral injury, trauma, or chronic suffering associated with blaming God for these situations, can lead to your love for Jesus dying.

You probably have seen this in the marriage of someone you've known; maybe even in your own family. The parties may be "going through the motions"…living together; going about their daily routines…but love is no longer the motivator; the comfort associated with the routine *is*. The kids get fed and the dishes get washed, but the love in the marriage and the love in the home, is gone. Children know it when it happens to their parents and it's not just sad; it's almost always *devastating* to them. Their parents stop talking, other than the token, cursory salutations. They stop performing loving gestures for one another, and eventually, they stop loving one another. Their feelings become lukewarm toward each other and they become indifferent; not really caring what the other one does or even, if they exist. Their love dies, but *only* because they let it die. This "lukewarm" frame of mind is a choice.

Lots of people still go through the motions in their spiritual life, too, even though their love for Jesus has waned; they go to church every Sunday; they sing the songs. They may even raise their hands during worship, indicating that this particular "praise phrase" really means something to them. But the truth is, it only used to. It doesn't mean anything anymore if the love is gone.

Or, maybe you've never had a deep love for Jesus in the first place. In the United States and in the rest of the world, there are millions of people who claim to be Christians. They believe this because their family members are Christians or because Christianity is the most accepted and supported "religion" of the social culture. Although the support of Christianity has been rapidly deteriorating in the United States, it's still thought of as the most socially acceptable "religion" in many areas of the country.

If your Christianity is something you lay claim to merely by way of association, though, you are the epitome of being "lukewarm" toward Jesus. If you believe, like many so-called Christians, that there are "many paths to God and Jesus is just one of them," you are lukewarm. Why would Jesus have come to the earth as a man, shown His status as God by healing people and resurrecting the dead, then go to a torturous death on the cross, if it were possible for you to make it to heaven by believing in Buddha? And if you were Jesus and you went through all of that to take back authority from the devil and save billions of souls, how would you feel about those who, by way of their lukewarm attitudes toward you, render your work and your sacrifice, to have been made in vain?

Maybe you just think of yourself as being more closely aligned with Christianity than any other religion. This is not good enough for Jesus, either, because Jesus is *alive,* and He's looking for those who want to have a relationship with Him.

Being lukewarm is a choice; a decision that can be made due to wrong priorities (thinking of anything and everything else as more important than Jesus, even the pettiest aspects of daily life). Sometimes people make the poor choice of being indifferent toward Him because they wrongly believe this will protect them. They can't tolerate the peer pressure or social ridicule that may come from being "a devout Christian" or they're afraid of the attacks of the devil.

Being lukewarm means that they have decided to turn their heart away from the Lord and you have deliberately chosen to be indifferent, lacking concern or interest in the Lord.

If you have chosen to turn your heart away from Jesus, for whatever reason; if you've become lukewarm toward Him…your choice has not been the right one.

If you were once on fire for Jesus, but through the process of time, let your love for Jesus die, then how are you any better than the masses of the unbelieving world - those who go on with their lives thinking about their jobs, their friends, spouses, children, maybe where the next party's going to be, but not much else? They give Jesus little thought at all. The world is full of these people.

Being lukewarm also means you are capricious. You can easily be swayed one way or the other, whichever way the culture goes, or whichever way you "feel on any given day." You could even let go of God altogether if the pressures of hardship, or social pressures, get to be too much for you. This happened repeatedly to the Israelites. They grew lukewarm toward God, then became so capricious – so easily led astray – that they took up worship of Baal and other false idols. After all God had done for them – parting the Red Sea, bringing them out of their Egyptian enslavement, etcetera, etcetera! They continued to reject Him. And the Bible says that their lukewarm attitudes were offensive to God.

When my family members went through a long period of tragedy upon tragedy, I became so angry with Jesus. I kept telling Him, "How could you let all these things happen to us? We were faithful. We were all following You! And I, I was madly in love with (my heart was on fire for) you! How could You?" I felt a particular resentment because of all my son had to go through. "He's only a child!!" I would say to the Lord, in case He needed me to point that out to Him. Apparently, He had forgotten. "How could You let him go through so much devastation?" For a long time, I just couldn't believe it, until eventually, my shock and dismay turned to anger toward Him.

I'm not saying my attitude was right; it wasn't. I knew it wasn't right. I was unequipped to change it by myself. However, according to Jesus' own words, my coldness (anger) was better than letting my love toward Him die off completely. I never stopped loving Him; I knew better than to allow that to happen.

Whenever I thought about Him, tears would still come to my eyes. I longed to return to that time when I was a young believer; when He poured His Spirit over me night after night, telling me things from His word and just being with me. His Presence is the most wonderful paradise there is, in and of itself, and I wanted to go back there and live in that time, once again. I longed for His Presence and His favor to return to me.

According to Jesus in Revelation 3:16, allowing your love for Him to grow lukewarm is a very dangerous place to be. It means you just don't care anymore…if you ever truly did. Maybe you don't care about this world, but never let yourself adopt that attitude toward Jesus. It's imperative that you don't allow that to occur, and if it has already, that you get back to being hot (or even cold) for Jesus!

Your love for Jesus is worth finding, or if you knew it and it went cold, it's worth resurrecting. Your love for Jesus is worth protecting. Do not let it die. To Him, this is devastating and offensive after what He went through to save you.

Give Careful Thought:
If you are in a state of being lukewarm toward the Lord, ask Him to change your heart right away. Ask Him to forgive you for your period of indifference and to light the fire in your heart again (or for the first time) toward Him. Ask for any loss of love for Him that you've experienced to be restored; that your passion for Him and for His word, would be reignited, never to be lost again.

9

Suddenly

I suffered with chronic, excruciating pain from spinal stenosis for eight-and-a-half years as a result of complications from chemotherapy treatments. I was receiving the chemotherapy while in a clinical trial treatment program for breast cancer. During those years of immense pain, I prayed constantly for Jesus to heal me. I knew He could. After the months turned into years of almost unbearable pain, I grew to believe that either He didn't want to heal me, or there was some purpose for my pain. One day I heard a pastor say, "Stop placing your own mental objections between you and your healing. Jesus wants to heal you; He does not have a purpose for your pain." Since it seemed like this pastor was "reading my mind," and because I didn't believe in coincidences, I felt that the Holy Spirit was the One responsible for this message coming to me, and I believed it. Then, suddenly, I was healed. That was six years ago.

In the Bible there's a story about chronic suffering, but God ended it suddenly; in one day. 2 Kings Chapters 6-7 tells the story of when the King of Aram laid siege to Samaria and the siege lasted a very long time. Everything good, including daily provisions, had been withheld from the Samarians until their plight became desperate. However, Elijah's successor, Elisha, heard from the Lord that within 24 hours the long-time siege would be lifted, the people would be delivered out of their longtime poverty and drought. And that is exactly what happened.

2 Kings 7:1: *"Elisha said, 'Hear the word of the LORD. This is what the LORD says: About this time tomorrow, a seah of flour will sell for a shekel and two seahs of barley for a shekel at the gate of Samaria."*

The king's assistant doubted this could happen.

2 Kings 7:2: *"The officer on whose arm the king was leaning said to the man of God, "Look, even if the LORD should open the floodgates of the heavens, could this happen?"*

The story goes on to tell us how four lepers who were starving, devised a plan to go over to the camp of the Arameans and turn themselves in to the enemy. They were so desperate in Samaria, they had nothing to lose. They determined that even if the Arameans killed them, their fate would be no worse than if they stayed in Samaria where there was no food or water; where they were about to die of starvation anyway. So, they traveled over to the enemy camp and snuck up on them. This is what happened:

2 Kings 7:5-8
"At dusk they got up and went to the camp of the Arameans. When they reached the edge of the camp, no one was there, **6** *for the Lord had caused the Arameans to hear the sound of chariots and horses and a great army, so that they said to one another, 'Look, the king of Israel has hired the Hittite and Egyptian kings to attack us!'* **7** *So they got up and fled in the dusk and abandoned their tents and their horses and donkeys. They left the camp as it was and ran for their lives.*

⁸ The men who had leprosy reached the edge of the camp, entered one of the tents and ate and drank. Then they took silver, gold and clothes, and went off and hid them. They returned and entered another tent and took some things from it and hid them also."

Eventually, the men realized their responsibility to tell the king of Samaria of their findings and the entire city was rescued by the plunder of their enemies. All but one. The king's assistant, the one who had doubted, didn't make it. In the stampede of the people who were in a rush to get to the supplies, he was trampled to death at the city gate. The Bible makes this point again and again: faith in God and in His word is important to Him, and there can be real consequences for disbelief.

In Luke Chapter 5, Simon Peter had been fishing all night to no avail, and he was exhausted. Jesus told him to go out into the "deep water," put his net back into the lake and try, one last time, to catch something. The disciples had given up, but when Jesus gave Peter this instruction, Peter followed it. With Jesus' direction and Peter's obedience, there was a much different result. The net became so full that it began to break. In their own strength and power, the disciples could catch nothing, but with Jesus all things are possible.

Whatever your "hope deferred" may be, Jesus is the answer. You may or may not get a *sudden* answer to your prayer, but even if you've asked for years to no avail, keep asking. And keep praising Him.

Give Careful Thought:
Sometimes the Lord moves suddenly like He did for the Samarians in 2 Kings, but it took faith.
When the time is right, Jesus will heal you and your hopes will be fulfilled. If you have little hope, little ability to believe the above

statement, and little strength left, ask Jesus to help you with these things. You can even ask Him to help you if you're lacking faith.

Don't give up. Keep asking. Keep putting one foot in front of the other and keep going.

Psalm 103:5
"He satisfies your desires with good things, so that your youth is renewed like the eagle's."

10

Not So Fast!

When God Withholds

Hannah was a young wife who suffered for years due to God withholding from her the most coveted position in ancient Jewish culture: that of motherhood. Just as many in our culture today believe material prosperity represents God's blessings on a person's life (which is a misperception), having children meant God's blessing was on your life to the Israelites at Hannah's time. The general view was: the more children you had, the greater God's blessing was upon you.

Yet, the Lord withheld children from Hannah for years. The Bible says:

"...Elkanah, Hannah's husband, had two wives; one was called Hannah and the other Peninnah. Peninnah had children, but Hannah had none."
1 Samuel 1:2

In addition to the pain of having a deep, unfulfilled desire for children year after year, in that culture Hannah's childless state brought with it humiliation. Along with believing children meant God's blessing, the ancient Jews also believed that if you didn't have children, God's curse must be upon you. If that wasn't disappointing enough, it must have seemed as if God was playing some kind of cruel joke on Hannah when her rival, Peninnah, tormented her because of her childless condition:

"And because the LORD had closed her womb, her rival kept provoking her in order to irritate her. This went on year after year. Whenever Hannah went up to the house of the LORD, her rival provoked her till she wept and would not eat."
1 Samuel 1: 6-7

To make matters even worse, Hannah's self-centered husband, Elkanah, thought *he* was the answer to her problems:

"Why are you downhearted? Don't I mean more to you than ten sons?"
1 Samuel 1:8

He thought she should be happy just to have him, even though the entire culture looked upon a woman without children as cursed. Hannah was, no doubt, shunned and ashamed, feeling alone and unsupported, wondering why God had forsaken her. In fact, I think Hannah may have had thoughts such as: "Really, God? This woman (her rival, Peninnah) is mean, vengeful, and corrupt to the core, and yet, You give her Your blessings of many children. I'm good in heart, faithful to You, and trying my best to follow and obey You, yet You curse me by blocking me from having children. What did I do to deserve Your curse? Don't you care about me, at all?"

The unfairness of it all must've overwhelmed Hannah at times.

Hannah took her issue to the Lord; right into the temple, into the presence of Eli, the priest. She moved her lips as she prayed silently, causing the priest to think she was drunk.

"And she made a vow saying "'O LORD Almighty, if you will only look upon your servant's misery and remember me, and not forget your servant but give her a son, then I will give him to the LORD for all the days of his life, and no razor will ever be used on his head.'"
1 Samuel 1:11

So, the Bible says, in the course of time, Hannah conceived and gave birth to a son who she named Samuel. Hannah lived up to her part of the bargain and dedicated him to the LORD. Samuel grew up to be a judge and prophet of God whose events are chronicled in 1st and 2nd Samuel. He called the Israelites to leave their idol worship and return to the God of Israel again and again. God even used him to call out the evil sons of Eli who were corrupt priests in the temple.

Not only that, but God brought justice to Hannah for all the evil taunting of her enemy:

"She who was barren has borne seven children, but she who has had many sons pines away."
1 Samuel 2:5(b)

Hannah's entire prayer of praise is written in 1 Samuel, Chapter 2, but I especially love verses 6-10:

"The LORD brings death and makes alive;
  he brings down to the grave and raises up.
7 The LORD sends poverty and wealth;

he humbles and he exalts.
8 He raises the poor from the dust
   and lifts the needy from the ash heap;
he seats them with princes
   and has them inherit a throne of honor.
"For the foundations of the earth are the LORD's;
   on them he has set the world.
9 He will guard the feet of his faithful servants,
   but the wicked will be silenced in the place of darkness.
"It is not by strength that one prevails;
10 those who oppose the LORD will be broken.
The Most High will thunder from heaven;
   the LORD will judge the ends of the earth.
"He will give strength to his king
   and exalt the horn of his anointed."
1 Samuel 2: 6-10

During the years that Hannah suffered the scourge of being barren and the humiliation that brought within her community as well as the constant tormenting of her enemy, God was doing something that resulted in His plan being fulfilled: Samuel was born and dedicated to the Lord. Even as a young boy God spoke to him. The Bible says he grew in stature and favor with the Lord and men (1 Samuel 2:26). Eventually, because Samuel was pure of heart before the Lord and Eli and his sons were not, God used him to call down a curse on the house of Eli. Samuel was called upon to anoint David king when he was just a kid and Saul was still in power (1 Samuel 16:13). And everything God spoke through Samuel was fulfilled.

Hannah went down in history as someone the Lord favored; someone the Lord trusted with the incredible privilege of giving birth to one of the major prophets of the nation of Israel and of the Bible. In addition, God also entrusted Hannah with the immense responsibility of dedicating Samuel to God, then giving him to the priests to raise so that he would have the training and preparation he would need to meet his calling. Ever since these events were written down, all of mankind has been privy to this story of God temporarily withholding something valuable because He had a plan to rescue a nation from their idol worship.

God also withheld children from Abraham and Sarah, for decades, and we all know how that story unfolded. For years and years God withheld the most treasured blessing known to man at the time – children - from Abraham's and Sarah's union. All the while, God kept promising them that He would cause them to have so many children they would number the stars in the sky, and that the blessing of Israel, and the world, would come from their offspring.

During the time in which God withheld their promised child, Sarah became so discouraged she turned to the sin of self-sufficiency to try and solve their problem of childlessness. Sarah suggested that Abraham have a baby with her maidservant, Hagar. The child produced out of that union, Ishmael, became the source of the conflict over the Promised Land of Israel to this day. Ultimately, that long-awaited child brought forth by the Lord to Abraham and Sarah – their child, Isaac – brought about the blessings to the entire world which God had promised Abraham and Sarah. Through Isaac came the twelve tribes of Israel, the Jewish nation, and eventually, The Messiah.

"Against all hope, Abraham in hope believed and so became the father of many nations, just as it had been said to him, "So shall your offspring be."
Romans 4:18

In my own life, I had my own idea for my own path, and that track was professional success, i.e.: I had my own track in mind for professional executive positions and business ownership. I was good at what I did, and made a lot of money for a lot of other people, and I was determined to proceed down this path. However, God would not prosper me, no matter what I did. The best business plans with the best-planted seeds would never succeed. Following each failure; each loss; my initial reaction would be shock because I couldn't understand: if I could make so much money for other people, I must know what I'm doing. So why then, would God not allow me to make any money for myself and my family?

Then, after I lost everything time and time again, God showed me that *His plan* for my life (my God-Track) was not the same as *my plan* for my life. He showed me that He was withholding success and all financial gain from me on the path that I pursued because I wasn't on the right track. Over the course of time, the Lord showed me that there was only one path for me that had His favor and His blessing – it was for me to write, telling the stories of what He has done in my life, in order to praise and glorify Him.

Had I been successful in business, pursuing my own self-centered path, you would not be reading about ways to have your hope resurrected now. Instead, through fulfillment of my God-Track, many have come to a belief in Christ through the books God inspired and prompted me to write. Many more have found new hope. My God-Track, which was pre-planned and pre-ordained by the Lord, has proven to be much more spiritually fruitful than anything I could've planned for myself, despite the confusion and frustration, even anger, through which it was forged. While God was withholding good things from me, He had a plan in mind. And even if only *one person* in this world was inspired to receive Jesus Christ through something I wrote, or if only one person's hope gets restored because he or she read about Hannah, Abraham and Sarah, or my God-Track journey; that one soul is priceless in value to the Lord. *You* are priceless to the Lord.

You are worth more to God than all the businesses and all the money in this world. That is how much God loves you and how much you mean to Him: everything.

It may be humanly impossible to withstand the internal and even the societal pressures that come when God withholds something from us for a long time. But with God, all things are possible. He will uphold you while you stand against those pressures.

Has God promised you something that you've waited a long time for, causing you to lose hope that it will ever happen? If so, I pray right now that the Lord of Heaven and Earth will come through and deliver you into the "Promised Land." May you have the longing of your heart, or even better – may you find and fulfill your God-Track; God's plan for your life. Until that day, may you have God-given strength to stand while you wait. Amen.

If the Lord continues to withhold something He has promised you, the waiting period can be fraught with frustration and confusion. Just remember – the Bible says:

"...*so is my word that goes out from my mouth:*
   It will not return to Me empty,
but will accomplish what I desire
   and achieve the purpose for which I sent it."
Isaiah 55:11

Sometimes, God's plan requires preparation and testing in order to bring about something very special (i.e.: the prophet Samuel through Hannah or the nation of Israel through Abraham and Sarah, including the ancestral line of Jesus Christ). No matter how long you've gone with a longing unfulfilled; no matter how long you've waited and wondered where God is, you need to know that God's plan for you is better than your plan for yourself. Trust God. Have faith in His goodness. It may be that you're about to see something prodigious occur. And if it doesn't happen here, when He comes back, (and He's coming soon), your life will be better than you could ask or imagine because you will be in His Presence forevermore.

Give Careful Thought:
If you've had a promise from God for something in your life and God has withheld it from coming to pass, remember that God always keeps His promises. He cannot lie. Therefore, like Hannah, Sarah, and Abraham, you may have been called to a prolonged time of preparation and testing, too.

If it is appropriate for you, try praying this prayer:
Lord Jesus, please renew my hope and refresh my faith in Your promises for me. Please give me the wisdom and strength to stay the course if You continue to withhold the promise from me. Please help me obey You and allow You to mold me in preparation for Your calling on my life.

If there is something that you've lost…a business, a financial blessing, health, or a person who meant a lot to you in this life who has gone on to be with the Lord…remember that God is for you and He will never leave you. This life is not all there is, and as long as you have faith in Jesus Christ as your Lord and Savior, and your loved one(s) had faith in Him, you will see them again in heaven. When you do, you'll not only be reunited forevermore, but we will all be united with the Lord Jesus for eternity. There is no other place in this universe or beyond that is better, or that can offer you more than heaven and being with the Lord can.

Getting to that blessed place is what we ought to hope for most of all.

11

God Knows

If you feel that God hasn't been there for you; that He isn't paying attention to you; that He has forgotten you or for some other reason has left you alone…you need to know – He hasn't.

In some of the later chapters we're going to talk more about that feeling – that God has abandoned you. We'll discuss in more depth the phases God may take you through in preparation for you to get on your God-Track.

Every tear that you've cried, God knows. Every minute of anguish and despair, He has felt right along with you. Even when you believed He no longer cared, He did.

Some of the first verses in Haggai are about God telling the Jews that He knows about their needs. He recognizes how much their lives have been lacking.

"You have planted much, but have harvested little. You eat, but never have enough. You drink, but never have your fill. You put on clothes, but are not warm. You earn wages, only to put them in a purse with holes in it."
Haggai 1: 6

"How does it look to you now? Does it not seem to you like nothing?"
Haggai 2:3

God knew exactly what the Jews were thinking and feeling, all along. He knew their situation down to each lacking kernel of wheat. Have you come to believe that God either doesn't know your need, or that He forgot? It may surprise you to know that God knows exactly what you've longed for and exactly what you need. He hasn't forgotten about it or about you. He remembers.

Validation is a human need. We all want to have our thoughts and feelings reinforced by someone we respect. Every one of us looks for this in our relationships. Without it, we truly feel alone in this world. By being with other people who care enough to understand us and who respect our thoughts and feelings, we feel more valued and more alive.

In fact, I've drawn away from people who seem to ignore or negate everything I say and I have, instead, sought out friends and support from people who respect what I think and feel. My closest friends and family members listen to me as I express my feelings and opinions, and even if they don't agree with me, they express that they care. They aren't "yes-men" but they offer respectful understanding, even if they choose to also offer me a different way of looking at the issue. This describes healthy interaction among people who value one another.

Your desire to know that God knows and understands what you've gone through and respects your feelings is healthy and natural. It boils down to having a desire to be known by God and to have Him care about you.

In Haggai, God points to some factors that have blocked the fulfillment of His promises to the Israelites. After years of wondering while God had been withholding good things from them, God finally spoke to them, validating that He was there, and that He knew the hardships they had been experiencing. God even explained to them what had been happening so they could understand it better, and then He encouraged them with direction and promises. We'll get into these scriptures more in the coming pages but, for now, I want you to realize that God knows what you've been going through, and He is for you; He is on your side. It's imperative that you have faith in this. How else can you have a relationship with Him?

My pastor once said from the pulpit, "Without God, in this world there would be *nothing good at all!*" God is always good, even when life isn't.

Some time ago, I was verbally attacked by two of my closest friends, within a couple months of each other. Each of these attacks was vicious. They couldn't have come at a worse time – I was already dealing with low self-worth and feeling like my life was nothing but one giant, epic failure. My emotions were already raw. I was so upset. It was like being kicked when I was already down.

It was during this period of raw pain and lowly hopelessness that the Lord spoke to me. While I was praying, into my head came a Scripture book and verse from Job. When I opened up my Bible and read the passage, I was amazed to be reading my own story right there on the page.

"My friends treat me with scorn,
as my eyes pour out tears to God."
Job 16:20

Just knowing God cared enough for me to give me that scripture, meant He was listening to me when I was crying out. It meant He was there and He cared….and that meant everything to me. Despite the fact that I'd felt either forgotten (at best) or smote (at worst) by Him, at lease I now knew He hadn't left me.

As I read on, I read about how God was upset with Job's friends for what they'd done to him; attacking him when he was so down in his spirit. They had accused Job of being the one who was at fault for all that had happened to him, just as my friends had done to me. They told Job he was to blame for causing his own problems; that it was his sin that was the source of all of his calamities.

That was not true. God had allowed satan to attack Job, but not because Job had sinned and offended God. God was not angry with him.

When my years of desiring to have professional success (even to just get by and make a living) had been thwarted by God, I knew that He was causing the obstruction. I used to tell friends this all the time: "God is the one doing this!" I would repeatedly say. Many people fell away from me because they either thought that I was at fault and that my blight was occurring due to my own sin; that I was in denial about myself; and/or that I was wrongly blaming the Lord. However, God was saying something different to me.

God vindicated Job because He let him know that all that he had been through, all that he'd lost, was not due to sin or any fault of his. In fact, many have suggested that God let satan attack Job because God was proud of him. Job was not to blame for all that had occurred and I felt the Lord was saying the same thing to me; that I was not to blame!

Knowing that God was there with me had been a huge validation to me that He did, indeed, care about me and hadn't forgotten me. In fact, God cared enough to speak to me right out of His word precisely concerning those things that I'd been crying out to Him about. He told me that I wasn't to blame for the bad things that had happened to us. This was a huge turning point for me in my life. Suddenly, I felt lighter, as though I'd been relieved of a heavy burden I'd been carrying around for so long.

God purposefully made you and He's had a plan for your life all along. Your life has meaning and value, so much so that you were created to do something on this earth that no one else can do. That's how important your life is and how imperative it is that you find your purpose and fulfill it.

This book will help you do that. For now, it's crucial that you know that God is Love, He created you in love, and He ultimately wants only good to come to you. Why, then, has bad come into your life? There are many possible reasons for this. Some of which may include things that you're at fault for: poor judgment, a lack of maturity, a poor attitude. Or, as we've already established in the preceding chapters, it's possible that you've had something you've been hoping for withheld because God has been guiding you through a period of preparation and/or testing. Through it all, God knows.

We have to remember that we live in a fallen world; one in which satan and his fallen angels have dominion over the unbelieving world. That has to affect us because we live here, too! So, of course, as the culture deteriorates further and further into hedonism…as evil is on the rise…we have no choice except to experience some of the consequences of that evilness. While you have a lover of your soul, you also have an enemy who wants to do you harm.

Nevertheless….do not fear. The power of God created billions and billions of stars just by breathing them into existence. The Bible says that once you put your faith in Jesus Christ and what He did for you and for me on the cross, He took back over the lives of every believer. The devil no longer you. God Himself took back all power and and placed it in the loving hands of Your

authority over you a
holds power over
dominion ov

Redeemer. Have faith that God not only has the power to bless you and restore you, but that He also *wants* to.

Give Careful Thought:
Pray this prayer: Lord, You know all that I've been through. At times I've felt like You were nowhere to be found. At times I've felt like You may have known what I was dealing with, but You must not have cared.

Please help me see that You know all about my circumstances and what I've been going through. You are with me and You understand. Please help bring me up out of the mire, Lord.

I know that You are sovereign and have the power to change my life, but I've grown to doubt your desire to help me, especially in the area of:

_____

_____

_____

_____

Lord Jesus, I want to believe now that You have heard my prayers, that You understand the cry of my heart, and that You will bring about the restoration I need. Please help me, Lord, even where I lack belief that Your intentions toward me are good. Jesus, please let me know that You hear my prayer. Amen.

Meditate on these Scriptures:

Mark 9: 22-24

"But if you can do anything, take pity on us and help us."
"If you can?" said Jesus. "Everything is possible for one who believes."
Immediately the boy's father exclaimed, "I do believe; help me overcome my unbelief!"

Matthew 19:26

"Jesus looked at them and said, 'With man this is impossible, but with God all things are possible.'"

Job 19:25

"I know that my redeemer lives,
and that in the end He will stand on the earth."

Joshua 22:22

"The Mighty One, God, the LORD! The Mighty One, God, the LORD! He knows!"

Psalm 103: 1-6, 13-14

"Praise the LORD, O my soul;
all my inmost being, praise His Holy Name.
Praise the LORD, O my soul,
and forget not all His benefits –
Who forgives all your sins
and heals all your diseases,

Who redeems your life from the pit
and crowns you with love and compassion,
Who satisfies your desires with good things
So that your youth is renewed like the eagle's.
The LORD works righteousness
and justice for all the oppressed...

As a father has compassion on his children,
so the LORD has compassion on those who
fear Him;
for He knows how we are formed,
He remembers that we are dust."

12

You Have a God-Track

Haggai 1: 7 - 8
"This is what the Lord Almighty says: "Give careful thought to your ways. Go up into the mountains and bring down timber and build the house, so that I may take pleasure in it and be honored," says the Lord."

Jeremiah 29:11
"For I know the plans I have for you," declares the Lord, "plans to prosper you and not to harm you, plans to give you a hope and a future."

When the ancient Jews were released out of Babylon at Haggai's time, a selected group of them returned to Jerusalem. They had a very clear mandate and they knew what it was: to rebuild the Temple so that worship of the One-and-only True God, the God of Israel, could resume there. However, their enemies had their own intended purpose: to stall, and eventually stop altogether, the temple-build project.

When the enemies of the Jews assailed them with attacks, they fought back and kept their faith in God's goodness for a few years. They kept pushing through the struggles, building the temple as they were instructed to do by the Lord…but the vicious attacks from their enemies continued with no end in sight. Eventually, the Jews became so afraid and bewildered; the building of the temple came to a standstill.

Once the returning remnant laid aside the temple build project, things got even worse for them in the way of drought, scourge, and blight. By the time God speaks to them through Haggai, He tells them that it has been Him Who has been blighting their resources because He hasn't been happy with their choice to stop fulfilling their God-mandated purpose.

The returning remnant may have had thoughts like this: "God, You delivered us out of Babylon, returned us to our home, and this is what we get for being the ones who were willing to come back here and rebuild the temple? Why didn't You protect us more? Why did You allow these things to happen to us?"

We can glean lessons from Haggai and what happened to the Israelites way back then. First of all, we can understand that God has a plan and purpose in mind for each of us. Secondly, we can see that the God-Track the Lord had spelled out for the Jews was very specific. While they were fulfilling it, things may have been difficult, but when they weren't fulfilling it things were even worse. We have an enemy, and he can wreak havoc on our lives…but not obeying God can bring about even greater consequences for us than enemy attacks can. That's what happened to the returning remnant.

Let's focus for a moment on how those ancient Jews got into their predicament – where God was scourging and blighting everything in their lives. First, they got discouraged from the horrible attacks of their enemies. They began to feel so much fear that they then began to doubt that they really needed to fulfill their God-mandate.

These feelings of doubt and fear are human. If you've felt them toward God, it's okay. You and I have a spiritual enemy while living here on earth, and he can bring about a lot of upset, stress, and confusion into our lives. He hates you already, but he especially hates Christians because it is only God who can control our destiny; not him. He hates it most when a former non-believer becomes a believer. Your spiritual enemy hates to give up souls (or "ground" or "land") that he claimed for himself. Most of all, he hates it when we worship God.

Attacks from the enemy can come in many forms of strife, causing depression, loneliness and hopelessness in our lives. Maybe you, or even your child, have been bullied in school or on social media. Maybe you have been the victim of a horrible crime and you've had trouble recovering from it. Have you had financial distress that just seems as if it will never relent? Do you suffer physically, badly needing a healing in your body; possibly suffering with a disease that's plagued you for years?

What's important is that you don't get stuck in the paralyzing effects that these feelings of bewilderment, disappointment, and doubting God, can cause.

In Haggai, God explained to the Israelites why their lives had been lacking in every area, and He gave them specific instructions for how to end the blight in their lives. He told them to get back to building the temple (their anointed, God-given purpose; their God-Track). This was the only way out of their despair.

I'm not saying that your life-blight or crushed hope has been your own fault, as it came to be for the returning remnant. What I am saying is that the answer to pulling your life out of hopelessness lies in finding and fulfilling your God-mandated life's purpose, just as it was the answer for the returning remnant.

When you know you have a purpose and you're working on fulfilling it, you have hope. Having purpose in your life gives your life the meaning and value God intended it to have.

I have a sister who became a Christian around the same time I and several of our other family members did. Once she read the Bible and understood what God expected of her, she turned toward Him and never looked back. She straightened up her life and really turned away from sin. She got married and she and her husband have regularly attended church for the past twenty years. My sister took excellent care of both of my parents when they were in the last days of their lives. She quit smoking cigarettes and hasn't had a drink of alcohol in all this time.

While living this "cleaned-up" life, however, my sister and her husband, who also came to the Lord, have had one spiritual attack after another. Her husband was almost killed in a motorcycle accident and has been disabled with chronic pain ever since it happened. My sister also had breast cancer and suffered for years from the ensuing treatments and complications, which greatly deteriorated her health. While their faith stayed strong, they went through financial devastation and lost their home. They have lost three of their four parents as well as several beloved dogs. It seems like they've had too much grief and unrelenting pain; yet my sister continues to inspire me with her faith and resilience.

On the other hand, after years filled with numerous tragedies…many of which also affected my son…I became downright indignant with God. God knew and I knew that during this period of my life, I was unqualified from fulfilling my God-Track. I could not tell others of God's goodness when I didn't think He was good, myself; at least not to me and my family members. So, my negative feelings of frustration and anger became an impediment to God using me the way He intended. I couldn't fulfill my life's purpose…my "God-Track"…because there were too many obstacles in the way, for me to do so. They've included anger, frustration, disappointment, materialism, selfishness, and fear. Therefore, just like the ancient Jews, I got stuck – paralyzed – in my wrong priorities.

However, over the course of time, God showed me what He wanted me to do. He showed me that I had a "God-Track" and the track was to write for Him in a way that would glorify Him. He showed me how He had instilled in me a gift for writing. He had placed these things in me going way back in my childhood; probably before my birth.

God also created you with a specific purpose in mind. He instilled gifts in you so you could accomplish the things He has ordained, from eternity, for you to accomplish. He needs you to fulfill this purpose; He needs you to fulfill your God-Track.

"This is what I covenanted with you when you came out of Egypt. And my Spirit remains among you. Do not fear."
Haggai 2:5

If you've had a period of suffering, know that it had a purpose and the purpose was to prepare, train, and test you so that you can do what you've been ordained and appointed to do. There's nothing in it for God, for others, or for the entire earth, for that matter, if your God-Track goes unachieved.

In the next few chapters I will tell you how God brought me to a knowledge of the truth about my own God-Track. I'll share with you the simple steps He took me through to help me find it. You can apply these same steps to your own life and find your God-Track, too; so let's get on with it.

Give Careful Thought:
Are you fulfilling the purpose for your life according to God's agenda? You have a "God-Track." If you get on it and serve out your purpose in Christ, you'll be surprised at how your degree of hope and the quality of your life will take a quantum leap forward.

Mediate on these Scriptures:

Psalm 20:4
"May He grant you according to your heart's desire, and fulfill all your purpose."

Psalm 90:17
"May the favor of the LORD our God rest upon us;
Establish the work of our hands for us –
yes, establish the work of our hands."

Haggai 2:4
"'Be strong and work. For I am with you,' declares the LORD Almighty."

Then, pray this prayer:

Father, I believe that You have a plan for my life and that plan is good. I believe you when Your word tells me that You have good intentions to bless me, even though I've waited a long time; even though I've thought it would turn around for so long, but have all but lost my hope that it ever will.

I recognize that I have a purpose for which You created me. That purpose is not about me. I lay the selfish desires of my heart down at Your feet. Please resurrect my hope and allow me to fulfill the purpose for my life, according to *Your* will.

Give my life purpose so that my hope is restored, please Lord. Show me the way to go. Amen.

13

Your God-Track
Is Very Specific

For many years I experienced financial distress and the stress it caused greatly diminished my quality of life; eventually making me nearly hopeless. It seemed like everything I did professionally, failed. And it did. You've heard of "The Midas Touch." I had the opposite; I had "The Blighted Touch." This long period of business failures and a chronic loss of jobs often caused periods of utter destitution, losses of homes, and even homelessness. My son and I were homeless several times.

Since I was educated and had strong business acumen as well as an unparalleled drive and determination, I couldn't understand why this was happening. It didn't make any sense.

During these years of constant financial blight, the Lord kept speaking to me out of Haggai:

Haggai 1:5-6:
"Now this is what the LORD Almighty says: "Give careful thought to your ways. ⁶ You have planted much, but harvested little. You eat, but never have enough. You drink, but never have your fill. You put on clothes, but are not warm. You earn wages, only to put them in a purse with holes in it."

Haggai 1: 9-10:

"You expected much, but see, it turned out to be little. What you brought home, I blew away. Why?" declares the LORD Almighty. "Because of my house, which remains a ruin, while each of you is busy with your own house. ¹⁰ Therefore, because of you the heavens have withheld their dew and the earth its crops. ¹¹ I called for a drought on the fields and the mountains, on the grain, the new wine, the olive oil and everything else the ground produces, on people and livestock, and on all the labor of your hands."

Through these verses, it seemed obvious to me what God was saying: God was telling me that He was blighting my finances Himself! It seemed as though He was also saying that He was doing this because I wasn't using my gifts, which had been instilled into me *by Him,* to build up His "house." I didn't know what God wanted me to do to help "build His house." Only through immense frustration and desperation, forged over a period of intense prayer, did God finally reveal my God-Track to me.

I worked hard at every job I had and every business I'd ever owned. I excelled and did a great job for many other business owners; making several of them millions of dollars. Nevertheless, on that track I wasn't anointed or blessed by God, because it wasn't the path He had created me to follow.

Proverbs 12:11 says:

"Those who work their land will have abundant food, but those who chase fantasies have no sense."

I knew Scripture; I knew the Bible said that if you plow, plant the seed, and diligently work the land, you will reap a great harvest. I tithed and followed Biblical principles, continued to "work the land," but still…no harvest. I saw other people – many of them – who didn't have half the work ethic that I had, who didn't seem to work as hard as I did, and others who were even unethical, but they were making money hand over fist. Still….for me?…..no harvest.

The problem was, I was plowing, planting, and working the *wrong land*! Therefore, I would work so hard to plow, carefully and lovingly plant and water the seed, care for the seed, work the land, then…..reap nothing. In fact, I would've welcomed nothing…..I reaped debt, failure, financial destitution and even homelessness for myself and my son. All of my "good works" amounted to less than zero, and all because I was on the wrong track.

According to Pastor Tim Storey, there's such a thing as a "good idea" and then there's a "God-idea." You must find the purpose for your life which God has appointed for you to do. You were made for nothing less.

If you feel like you've plowed and planted diligently and responsibly, but have yet to pull in a harvest from all of your hard work, you might also be on the wrong path for your life, as I was. You may be working the wrong land. Your calling is highly specialized; only you can do it. God planted gifts in you and developed you, even during your upbringing and through all of your pain, so that you can fulfill your purpose *in Him*! That's why your submission to Him is vital to your success.

"This is what I covenanted with you when you came out of Egypt."
Haggai 2:5

Your God-Track is the only path for you that God is going to bless. On your God-Track you'll have God's favor on you, on your work, and on your harvest. On your God-Track, you'll have God's grace on you and His word says He will bring abundance because you will be working the *right land*. Your God-Track is the only path that will bring you true joy and fulfillment, which comes not just from having a sense of purpose, but the deepest joy that can only come from fulfilling your *God-purpose*. Following your God-Track, you won't be able to lose hope because you'll know that you're doing what God has called you… and *only* you…to do.

Give Careful Thought:
Have you been planting much, but harvesting little? If so, it may be time to re-evaluate your path. Ask God to show you if you're on the wrong track (working the wrong land). If you feel confident that you're already on your God-Track, you can ask God to confirm that for you, and ask Him to give you the courage to fulfill it.

14

The Sun That Is Forgiveness

Forgiveness is an essential step you must take before you can find and fulfill your God-Track. It is also a crucial step in having your hope come back to you. As long as you hold onto a lack of forgiveness, you are diminishing your own power and God's power to work in your life. Some people say nothing can diminish God's power. But *you can*. You can limit His power in your life if you refuse to forgive someone; including yourself. This is a power associated with your free will.

Forgiving was one of the steps the Lord took me through while He was showing me that He had ordained a specific plan for my life. Whether or not I forgave was my choice, and whether or not I forgave determined the course I would be set upon.

Several years ago, I became homeless and ended up in a homeless shelter for women. I was completely devastated that my life had come to that. However, the experiences I had while residing there were things that the Lord used to ultimately set me on my God-Track.

After only a day there, one of my roommates named Tami, fell into tragedy. Her son shot himself in the head in an effort to commit suicide. When I found out about this from the other women at the shelter, I immediately went to the hospital to find Tami.

Tami's son, Kody, had survived the gunshot and was in critical condition. He had been rushed into surgery. After the surgeons removed the bullet from his brain, Kody was sent into the ICU and he stayed there for the next few weeks because the swelling in his brain had left his life hanging in the balance. Tami and I prayed constantly, as did many other people. Miraculously, Kody steadily improved until one day, about two months later, he was completely healed and walked out of the hospital. Kody was a walking miracle and even the medical professionals who had treated him acknowledged this.

I will never forget the trauma this episode caused Tami. She had been present at the time that Kody shot himself, watching the whole thing unfold. Kody had called Tami, crying in anguish as he told her of his intentions to shoot himself. She called the police; then rushed to his house. The police had arrived before she did and were talking to Kody through the front door of his house when she arrived. As a matter of protocol, though, the police locked Tami in the back seat of one of the patrol cars for her protection, precluding her from going up on the front porch to speak to Kody. Tami was sure that she could talk Kody out of taking that fateful step if she could just speak to him!

In his anguish, Kody told the police he was going to do it – shoot himself – that he just couldn't take the state of his life any longer. He then opened the front door stepping through it onto the front porch with a gun pointed at his head as Tami screamed from the back seat of the police car. Then, Kody shot himself right in front of the officers and his own mother.

Several days into this nightmare Tami was living through, while Kody lay unconscious in the ICU, Tami and I were assigned a new roommate. Her name was Renee.

Renee was a drug addict. The first night in our room, she woke me up at 2:45 a.m. as she was hyperventilating. As soon as I awoke I sat up in bed, wondering what that heavy breathing sound could be. Fuzzy-headed, I looked around the room and saw Renee standing by the door saying, "Oh, God…oh, God…oh, God."

Immediately I knew she was "nodding out" in her drug-induced state, while standing up. I assumed she didn't want to lie down because she didn't want to fall asleep and miss out on the hyper-euphoric stage of her high.

This infuriated me because I knew she was going to wake up Tami, who needed her sleep more than anyone I'd ever known to need sleep. She was still working, trying to hold onto her job through these events of Kody's life-threatening injury, and she spent all her waking hours at the hospital when she wasn't at work. Tami was having some long, exhausting days at that time.

And now, here was a drug addict being so inconsiderate that she was about to wake Tami up, because she was only concerned about her high. Sure enough, a few minutes later, that's exactly what happened. Tami woke up, a big hullabaloo took place and the whole big house was awakened. The police came.....but *eventually* everyone settled back down and went back to bed. Tami, however, lost valuable hours of sleep.

As for me, I just could not get over Renee's obscene selfishness; it was almost incomprehensible. As I've admitted many times, I wanted to punch Renee in the face; and then pepper-spray her, too.

Once Kody was discharged from the hospital, both Tami and I moved on and each found housing for ourselves. Life went on, and Tami and I stayed in touch.

About a year and a half later, I was struggling with anger and bitterness (more of it than I realized) and someone suggested to me that I should focus on forgiveness. I was so out of touch with myself I thought, "What forgiveness? Who needs to forgive? Not me." However, as I considered the suggestion more deeply, I realized it couldn't hurt to consider who I may need to forgive, and to work at it.

Over the course of that weekend, I kept seeing Renee's face...of all people's....in my mind. I knew this was from the

Lord because I thought I'd forgotten all about her, never giving her another thought after moving out of that shelter. Nevertheless, there she was, returning to my memory again and again. I soon realized why the Lord was bringing her to my mind. Each time I pictured her face in my head, I became enraged. I still wanted to punch that face, and I felt that if only I could have done that at the time of her hideous behavior, I would feel better *now*.

But the Bible says we are to forgive and let go of our need to exact vengeance ourselves; that is the Lord's job, as it says in Scripture:

*"Vengeance is Mine, and recompense; Their foot shall slip in due time; For the day of their calamity **is** at hand, And the things to come hasten upon them."*
Deuteronomy 32:35

"Beloved, do not avenge yourselves, but rather give room for God's wrath; for it is written, "Vengeance is Mine, I will repay," says the Lord."
Romans 12:19

I wasn't thinking of these verses at the time. I wasn't thinking that my act of forgiveness, if I could muster it, would have any effect on anything at all. I just knew Jesus was calling me to let go of this anger I felt toward a woman I didn't even know. The reason I was so angry with her was for the pain she had caused Tami, not me, anyway. So, I just kept seeing her face in my mind and saying to the Lord, "I forgive her, Lord, I forgive her." That was all I could do! In fact, the first several times I tried this, I still imagined punching that smug face of hers. Even though this was only happening in my imagination, it made me feel better. However, I knew that wasn't the exercise Jesus was calling me to, so I kept seeing her face in my mind and saying I forgave her, over the course of the entire weekend. Finally, sometime Sunday night, I felt some actual release come.

Monday came and went; then came Tuesday. Late that afternoon I turned on the television set. When a commercial came on for the six o'clock local news, the anchor presented the "tease" for the upcoming show. It was very short, but I thought I glimpsed the face of Renee flash up on the screen; the face that I had just been seeing in my mind that entire weekend! No... could it be?

I rewound the DVR and played the commercial over again. When I did, my question was confirmed – there was a picture of Renee's face up on the screen behind the news anchor as he explained the headline about a woman who had been charged with attempted murder. You can believe I didn't miss that news program. Apparently, Renee had gone into the hospital with a co-conspirator and administered a fatal dose of fentanyl to a patient there. The patient was a woman who, the authorities said, went into cardiac arrest and, were it not for the fact that she was already in the hospital, wouldn't have survived the attack. Renee had been caught trying to kill her. She was now charged with attempted murder, and was sitting in jail!

I called Tami right away and told her. We were both astounded at these events. One night of feeling furious toward someone led to a year-and-a-half of grudge-holding that I didn't even realize I held. Then, seeing Renee's face in my mind for an entire weekend led to seeing that exact, same face on the TV two days later. Finally, seeing that she was now in jail for attempted murder, and probably will be there for the rest of her life, or close to it. No one will *ever* be able to convince me that this set of circumstances amounted to a coincidence.

Through this experience, I also learned something about forgiveness that I'd never understood before. We tend to think

97

that the act of forgiveness as something we do just for our own emotional and psychological health. And forgiveness does offer those benefits. When I think about forgiveness I tend to think of "rainbows and ribbons;" this wonderful, gracious act that only results in peace and love. (I'm seeing heart emojis in my head right now.) I've often heard forgiveness described as an inward act that effects only the one who forgives. Forgiveness can result in healing and even reconciliation in relationships. Therefore, it can have, and often does, an effect on our physical world.

However, through *this* experience God showed me that my act of forgiveness can release *His judgment*. By forgiving, I gave up my "power" in the situation and handed it over to God to deal with…and boy, did He ever!

Forgiveness, and the lack thereof, can have significant spiritual *benefits and consequences* which can affect our lives in the real world, right away! Who would've thought?

When we forgive it releases the Lord to exact *His will*, sometimes displayed by His grace and mercy, and sometimes displayed by His judgment and justice on earth. In this particular case, that meant that Renee's evil behavior was exposed, she was caught, and she will now spend most, if not all, of the rest of her life in prison.

The Bible says that what we "loose" on earth will also be loosed in heaven. That includes forgiveness and any other act in which we tightly grip onto something we think we can control. What we bind on earth (control) we also bind in heaven (tie God's hands). Our hearts' desires and the actionable decisions and attitudes that we either cling to, or release, have an effect in the spiritual realm.

"Truly I tell you, whatever you bind on earth will be bound in heaven, and whatever you loose on earth will be loosed in heaven.

[19] *"Again, truly I tell you that if two of you on earth agree about anything they ask for, it will be done for them by my Father in heaven."*
Matthew 18:18-19

Give Careful Thought:
Is there someone that you need to forgive? Maybe even yourself?

Is it possible that by forgiving this person, your future could improve? For example, if you forgave them – someone who wronged you - maybe God would improve your circumstances? Maybe you would feel less bondage and more freedom. Maybe you would be happier. Maybe God would exact judgment on the other person now, or maybe not in this lifetime, but either way, you let the outcome go and trust God to handle it all.

And, since God says He will forgive you of all the mistakes and sins of your past, can you forgive yourself?

Pray this Prayer:
I ask You, Lord Jesus, please help me forgive anyone and everyone that I need to, including myself. Help me achieve the freedom that comes with the act of forgiving, and restore my hope for my future. And Lord, please show me if there is someone I need to forgive, of whom I'm unaware.

Lord, if there is any block in my life to your blessings, please reveal it to me. Please remove it. Fear, anger, an unforgiving spirit, or any wrong priorities such as materialism or other wrong motives – please remove any impediment to me fulfilling my God-Track. Thank You, Jesus. Amen.

15

Go Back

Haggai 2:15

"Now give careful thought to this from this day on – consider how things were before one stone was laid on another in the LORD's temple."

Haggai 2: 18-19

"...give careful thought to the day when the foundation of the LORD's temple was laid. Give careful thought: [19] Is there yet any seed left in the barn? Until now, the vine and the fig tree, the pomegranate and the olive tree have not borne fruit.
"'From this day on I will bless you.'"

One of the steps the Lord took me through to show me my God-Track was the process of "going back."

I discovered the life-transforming power of this step through Pastor Tim Storey and had it confirmed through the book of Haggai (in the Scriptures above). Pastor Storey explained that one step that is often effective in helping people find their purpose, is for them to go back in time to "the age of innocence" in their life. Doing so has helped many people, including me, find their God-given purpose.

Pastor Storey suggests going back to a young age in your life by using your memory. But when it's possible and practical to do so, he also suggests *physically* going back to a place where you spent significant time as a young child. That might mean visiting your old grade school (for example, go back there and sit on the swings) or going to the home you grew up in, while you "go back" to your childhood in your mind. Maybe you need to go sit in front of your grandparent's old house…just sit there for a while. Doing this should help you access memories from your childhood.

Warning: going through this exercise may elicit strong emotions. It's okay. Don't be afraid to experience them – your past is part of who you are and God wants to use it to help you. If you think it best, take a trusted friend or partner with you for support.

While you are on this quest of revisiting your childhood; going back in your memory to the "age of innocence," think about what it was you used to love to do in your youth. What dream had God placed in you, even back then?

After I had lost my first business and we were about to lose our second home, I wrote a book about Haggai and how I had felt like I'd been living it, for years. In reality, I sat down and wrote out of desperation; I didn't know what else to do to in order to be productive. Once it was finished, I gave a copy of that manuscript to my sister. She probably never read it (I admit it wasn't very good). It was finished, filed away in some box somewhere, and never thought about again. Meanwhile, I kept pursuing a professional track, and I kept on failing. However, three years later, when my sister was packing to move, she came across the manuscript and gave it back to me.

Shortly after that, I came across an interview with Pastor Tim Storey on the television one day. As I listened, he explained the concept of going back to the "age of innocence" and how it can help you access the gifts and the calling that God placed in you, which you probably became aware of at a young age.

I began thinking about my childhood; the home I grew up in and how I used to spend so much time in my room - *writing*. I suspected this was the method God was using to get my attention, because the book I had written and tried to give away, had just come back to me, seemingly out of nowhere.

What happened next was truly amazing. I was in the middle of reading "The Circle Maker" by Mark Batterson, at that time. In it, Batterson was telling how God qualifies us to do something when He calls us to it, even if we don't *feel* qualified to meet His call. I remember looking up, away from the page for a minute, and thought, "God, are you trying to tell me that You want me to rewrite that book I wrote about Haggai, years ago? I can't do that; what's the point? I have no formal education in writing, no established platform or audience, and I don't know anyone in the publishing business." But when I looked down at the next page, the very next words that I read were (paraphrased): "I tell this to aspiring writers all the time. If God has called you to write a book, don't worry about whether you're qualified to write, or whether you have a platform, or even whether you know anyone in the publishing industry."

Writing…Ding! Ding! Ding! The bells went off and the light bulb lit up in my head all at the same time! Again, I thought about how, as a kid, I would spend hours and hours alone in my room composing the most profound poems and songs, writing in my journal, and that for all of my life I'd had a fascination for words.

Well, now I understood why. God had placed that love for writing within me, and now He was telling me it was time to put that love to work.

Just like me, you have a God-Track; something God placed in you for you to do with your life. Before you were born, He had instilled it within you.

"Your eyes saw my unformed body;
  all the days ordained for me were
  written in your book
  before one of them came to be."
Psalm 139:16

A life with an unfulfilled purpose can be a hopeless life. A life lived on its God-Track is synonymous with a life filled with hope.

Steve Jobs said this:
"You cannot connect the dots looking forward; you can only connect them looking backwards. So, you have to trust that the dots will somehow connect in your future."

"I have filled him with the Spirit of God, with skill, ability and knowledge in all kinds of crafts – to make artistic designs for work in gold, silver and bronze, to cut and set stones, to work in wood, and to engage in all kinds of craftsmanship. Also, I have given skill to all the craftsmen to make everything I have commanded you."
Exodus 31: 3 – 6

Give Careful Thought:
God tells us through Haggai to "go back." This helped me, and according to Pastor Tim Storey, it has helped many others find their God-given purpose. You have a God-Track, and going back to your childhood may help you find it.

Try the exercise described in this chapter, and go back to the "age of innocence" in your life. If you can, physically return to your elementary school, your childhood home, or anywhere you used to spend a lot of time. Think carefully about what you used to love to do, or the dream you had in you, way back then.

Pray this prayer:
Lord Jesus, please show me my God-Track. If You placed within me certain gifts when You formed me, gifts You want me now to use to fulfill my purposes in You, please show me what they are and how You want me to use them. Amen.

16

Life-Crushing

This is the part of your walk with Christ you're not going to like. This is about the part of your story that hurts….but if I don't tell you about the crushing, I feel I'll be doing you a disservice.

Some Christian pastors and leaders preach only about the "blessings" that come from following God. They tell you that once you receive Jesus Christ you will experience only good things from that point on – healing, power, strength, prosperity, and happiness. They'll tell you that once you become a Christian your life will only get better. I call that the "Rosy Gospel." They don't want you to know about the cost of following Jesus because they don't want to scare you away from following Him. Their one-sided presentation of the Gospel is well-intended. However, I believe the church does an inadequate job of preparing new Christians for the life-crushing events that may come, as they preach only the Rosy Gospel.

It is typical that early in a believer's walk with the Lord, their circumstances may improve for a while as God displays His providence to them and solidifies their faith. However, experiencing an improved life and blessings *only* are not a guarantee in scripture. Some people experience no improvement in their circumstances whatsoever. Some see an improvement for a while, but then their life takes a nose dive as God takes them into the "refining fire," testing their faith, developing their character, maturing them, and preparing them for their God-

Track. Others experience hardship soon after they receive Christ and watch in shock as their lives get worse.

"...In this world you will have trouble. But take heart! I have overcome the world."
John 16:33

If you believe that everything in your life will only get better and better once you become a Christian, you may be unprepared for the troubles that will come while you're walking in God's will! If this happens to you, I don't want this to result in disappointments that take you down lower than they would have otherwise, just because your expectations for a better life were high. I don't want these disappointments to become so severe for you that you become hopeless.

Also, as I have explained in previous chapters, you have a spiritual enemy and he has a lot of power in this world. His throne was established here long before you came into existence. He will come against you because, at times, God will let him.

However, as a Christian, it is important that you understand two things, and these two things will create the "dynamic" you'll have in your relationship with God:

First....when you put your faith in Jesus Christ, you unequivocally did the right thing. You also angered the devil immensely because he wanted your soul to go to hell. Now it won't. Your faith in what Jesus did on the cross for you has now and forevermore sealed your eternal destiny. It also sealed your current status in the world. You are now a child of God and no one and no thing is more powerful than He is. So, while the devil will scheme, connive and try to manifest trouble for you, by placing your faith in Jesus Christ you took back the power satan

108

had over your soul and your life. You gave it back to the highest Power that exists – you gave all power over your life back to God. From that point forward, the devil can't do anything to you unless God allows it.

That brings us to the second point….the one that's sometimes hard for us to swallow: Bad things *will* happen to you here on earth – and once you're a Christian, everything that happens to you whether it is "bad" or "good," has gone through the filter of being okayed by God. Sometimes, God allows tragedies to happen to us, or He may withhold blessings, or "good" things from us (i.e. prosperity, just as He withheld it from the returning remnant at Haggai's time). In fact, if you look at the abuse and violence perpetrated against Jesus, His disciples, and the martyrs over the years, you realize that sometimes pain, injury, persecution and injustice are things that are within the will of God.

However, God *always* allows these abuses to occur for some greater purpose. And *always*, God allows these things to happen in the absence of malice. Despite the way it may look and feel, even sometimes for a long time, God only acts out of love. Always.

In order to test and prepare you for your calling, you may have to go through a "life-crushing" period. This period often is ordained by God because He needs to crush the carnality out of you, mature you spiritually, develop your character and test your faithfulness to Him through it, in order to prepare you for what He wants to accomplish through you.

Although life-crushing circumstances have a purpose, it can be very hard, even impossible, to see at the time they occur. Life-crushing situations may include strong feelings of confusion, disappointment, despair and diminished hope. It may even result in anger toward God. But if you take away nothing else from this chapter, I want you to remember this: the deeper your pain was, and the longer your period of longsuffering, the *greater is your calling.*

There are many examples in the Bible of people who endured life-crushings. Joseph was sold into slavery by his own brothers, then wrongly accused of rape and put in prison for over two years. But through the providential acts of God, Joseph eventually obtains so much favor from Pharaoh that he saves his estranged family and an entire nation from famine and annihilation.

Esther, Job, and the prophets endured life-crushing periods which they thought they could not bear. However, God held onto them, delivered them, and brought forth great deliverance for His people through them. Jesus' disciples and the early Christians also endured persecution as they stood for the Gospel, but due to their endurance billions of people have gone to heaven or are heaven-bound. (There are an estimated 2 billion Christians on the earth today.)

Give Careful Thought:
Please ask yourself this question: What is the one thing I need to know about the depth of my pain and the length of time I was in a period of life-crushing pain? The answer is on the previous page, middle paragraph, last sentence:

...the deeper your pain was, and the longer your period of longsuffering, the greater is your calling.

17

For Such a Time as This

When it comes to fulfilling your God-Track and the life-preparation that God invests in you to help you do so, you must also realize that God has an appointed time for you to fulfill your God-Track. He is the Master Planner and He not only has created you to fulfill a specific purpose, but to fulfill it at a certain time. When it comes to God and His plans, timing is everything.

Remember the story in Chapter 4 about Sue and the license plate that read: RAYHOPE? That story perfectly displays the importance of God's timing, and how He can orchestrate many different circumstances so they come to a head in the form of a miracle; just when you need it the most.

The Biblical story of Esther is one that points to the crucial factor of God's timing; one which led, once again, to the deliverance of the Israelites from utter extinction…just as God also did in the case of Joseph, for example.

The story of Esther is a beautiful love story; one of complicated circumstances that all divinely come together to save the Jews in the end.

Esther's parents die when she is young, and she is raised in Persia by her cousin, Mordecai.

When the king of Persia, King Xerxes, deposes his wife, Queen Vashti, because he is displeased with her, a search is done to find another queen. Esther, along with many other young women, is taken into the king's harem so that one of them can be selected to replace Vashti. As it happens, Esther is the one eventually chosen as the next queen of Persia. No one knows she is a Jew.

After Esther is made queen, her cousin Mordecai saves King Xerxes from a plot to assassinate him, which was being devised by his enemies. Mordecai told Queen Esther about the plot and she reported it to the king, giving credit to Mordecai.

The Bible explains that King Xerxes has as his primary official a wicked man named Haman, who despises the Jewish people. Haman is a descendant of Agag, an ancient Amalekite king. As the Israelites had journeyed from slavery in Egypt toward the Promised Land; the Amalekites had attacked them and tried to wipe them out. Once the Israelites gained control of the land, God commanded them to retaliate by annihilating the Amalekites, but the rebellious and disobedient King Saul disregarded the Lord's command and spared Agag (1 Samuel 15:9). This disobedience was now, all these years later, coming back to haunt the Jewish people as Agag's descendant, Haman, was plotting to wipe out the Jews, once again.

When the king orders all the people to honor and bow down to Haman, Mordecai refuses to do so, because he realizes who Haman is. This makes Haman's blood boil even more toward Mordecai and all of the Jews. So, Haman manipulates King Xerxes into issuing a decree which, when administered, will result in the extermination of every Jewish person living in Persia. The Bible never says that King Xerxes understands that the people about to be killed are the Jews, who are actually compliant with Persian laws and contributing members of society. Also, King Xerxes didn't know that his lovely new wife, Queen Esther, is Jewish.

However, Haman is successful in persuading the king to issue the decree through his skullduggery.

The edict goes out and the eradication of the Jews gets scheduled for an upcoming date. The people of Persia are perplexed, and the Jews are terrified.

Haman believes he has won this battle, once and for all, and that he's finally avenged his ancestors. But God has something else in mind.

Meanwhile, Mordecai recognizes the divine circumstances that exist; especially the way Esther had been raised up as queen, and there are hints in the story that he can see the broader picture. He persuades Esther to help; but she is also terrified because even the queen risks being executed if she approaches the king without being summoned by him. To initiate an approach to the king herself, Esther would be breaking the law, and just for placing this request, she knew she was risking her life. She tells Moredecai:

"All the king's officials and the people of the royal provinces know that for any man or woman who approaches the king in the inner court without being summoned by the king has but one law: that they be put to death unless the king extends the gold scepter to them and spares their lives. But thirty days have passed since I was called to go to the king."
Esther 4:11

However, Mordecai is convinced that Esther was placed in her position by God and His divine providence in order to save the Jews. He tells Esther:

"Do not think that because you are in the king's house you alone of all the Jews will escape. ¹⁴ For if you remain silent at this time, relief and deliverance for the Jews will arise from another place,

but you and your father's family will perish. And who knows but that you have come to your royal position for such a time as this?"
Esther 4:12

Esther has to make a life-or-death decision, and she proves herself to be a hero as she makes the right one:

"Then Esther sent this reply to Mordecai: ¹⁶ "Go, gather together all the Jews who are in Susa, and fast for me. Do not eat or drink for three days, night or day. I and my attendants will fast as you do. When this is done, I will go to the king, even though it is against the law. And if I perish, I perish."
Esther 4:15-16

By the time you finish reading the book of Esther, you can't help but see the hand of God in all of it. Everything turns around to bring about the deliverance of the Jews. Esther approaches the king and he gives her his favor; Haman's evil plot is uncovered and he is disgraced and executed; all of the Amalekites living in Persia are annihilated instead of the Jews; and finally, King Xerxes raises Mordecai to the highest position of all of his trusted officials.

While God is preparing you for your God-Track, He is planning and orchestrating events in order to bring about favor for you at just the right time, too. During this period of preparation, it may be necessary for you to stand in your faith; endure difficult circumstances; maybe even stare death in the face. Have faith in God's timing. Remember what Sarah did in her own self-sufficiency because she could wait for God no longer. Be careful that you don't make that same mistake. Wait on the Lord until He tells you it's time to move; you'll know when that is.

Give Careful Thought:
You may be in a period of preparation for your God-Track, too. If so, your God-Track will come about at just the right time: at "such a time as this." Become prepared; doing everything you can to obey God during this time, while you hold onto your faith.
Pray this prayer:
"Lord, if You have planned something for me to do at a future time; "for such a time as this"; please help me to be ready and prepared to fulfill my God-Track. Please help me to stand in my faith, endure hardship if You so ordain, and wait for Your divine timing. Amen."

18

Out of the Pit

Some people have found their God-Track only after being life-slammed with moral injury and atrocious tragedy. The family of Rachel Scott still speaks to crowds today, inspiring them with the story of her last words. Rachel was killed in 1999 by Eric Harris; one of the gunmen in the Columbine High School massacre. Rachel was known by her peers as a devout Christian. First, Harris shot her three times, in the chest, left arm, and left leg. Then he asked her, "Do you still believe in God?", to which Rachel replied, "Yes." Harris then shot her a fourth and fatal time in the left temple.

In the years following Rachel's death, her family started "Rachel's Challenge" and it became the most popular school assembly program in the U.S. The purpose of the program is to highlight Rachel's "Codes of Life" in order to affect change in people, and in communities across the nation. Rachel's primary moral value was compassion. She wrote an essay about this in her journal, one month before she was murdered.

Another well-known example of a person who took heinous tragedy and turned it into his God-Track is John Walsh. In 1981, he and his wife were at the center of one of the most shocking and unspeakable tragedies in U.S. history when their six-year-old son was kidnapped out of a shopping mall in Hollywood, Florida. Parts of Adam's body were found two weeks later about 100 miles from the mall.

It's impossible for most of us to even imagine the agonizing effects this horror story had on the Walsh family, but John Walsh turned this catastrophe into a life mission for himself; he found his God-Track. Walsh became a national spokesperson for victims' rights. He and his wife generated legislation to protect victims and impose stricter laws and punishments on child abusers, sex offenders, and other criminals; especially those perpetrated against children. They founded several child-abduction centers to assist in the searches and rescues of missing children, which were later merged with the National Center for Missing and Exploited Children.

If you live in the United States, you're undoubtedly aware of John Walsh as the host of the long-running reality crime show, "America's Most Wanted." In fact, many people worldwide are aware of John Walsh and his show. America's Most Wanted ran for over twenty years, showcasing current unsolved cases each week in which a suspect was on the run from law enforcement. The show led to the captures of over 1,000 fugitives. Who knows how many other families were saved from violent traumas because of the work John Walsh has done? God knows.

"Praise the LORD,
O my soul, and forget not all His benefits....
who redeems your life from the pit
and crowns you with love and compassion..."
Psalm 103:2, 4

No matter how low your life seems right now, God can redeem it from the pit and place a crown on your head, signifying His love and esteem for you. John Walsh assisted in the finding and rescue of Elizabeth Smart. There are other people out there who need your help, too. The Bible says God takes your circumstances, even tragedy and trauma, and turns them into something that is purposeful in helping the world be a brighter place.

"And we know that in all things God works for the good of those who love him who have been called according to His purpose."
Romans 8:28

"He who did not spare His own Son but gave Him up for us all – how will He not also, along with Him, graciously give us all things?"
Romans 8:32

God's own Son was murdered, too. Willingly. Don't forget that. He understands the pain the Walsh family went through better than anyone. And He will partner with you, if you'll let Him, to bring your life out of the pit and crown you with His love and compassion.

Give Careful Thought:
If you've been the victim of a crime or another tragedy, causing you to experience "moral injury' and/or severe psychological trauma, consider asking God to:

1) Heal you as only He can do – in your innermost being.

2) Send you someone, even several others, for the right support as you heal.

3) Help set your feet on "the Rock" and stabilize your life again.

4) And, lastly, show you how to turn your pain around and set you on the path that is your God-Track.

19

Settling the Issue
of Worthiness

God believes in you. He knows how you were formed; He knows every minute of your past…all your pain…and all of your weaknesses. And yet, He still believes in you. Who are you to try to override His opinion of you? You can't, even if you want to. You can't, no matter how hard you might try.

"As a father has compassion on his children,
so the LORD has compassion on those who fear   Him;
14 for He knows how we are formed,
He remembers that we are dust."
Psalm 103:13-14

God knew exactly what was in David's heart when He established him as the king of Israel. It was after David had become king that he made the monumentally poor decisions that led to adultery and intentional, pre-planned murder (2 Samuel 11). And David paid a high price for it, too (2 Samuel 12).

The Bible says that once God had taken David's newborn son, David got up and moved forward, despite his grief. He even went to the house of the Lord and worshipped:

"Then David got up from the ground. After he had washed, put on lotions and changed his clothes, he went into the house of the LORD and worshiped. Then he went to his own house, and at his request they served him food, and he ate."
2 Samuel 12:20

In his grief, David set his sights on eternity. He knew there was nothing he could do to bring back his dead child in this life. He knew he had sinned and displeased God terribly, and yet he knew he had a God-Track that he must fulfill. An entire nation's existence, security and prosperity depended on him. I believe this was a great turning point for David; one in which he turned from his self-centeredness and realized the tremendous responsibilities of his calling; one in which he finally decided to grow up. He knew his son was with God, and he would see him again in the next life:

"I will go to him, but he will not return to me."
[24] Then David comforted his wife Bathsheba, and he went to her and made love to her. She gave birth to a son, and they named him Solomon.
The LORD loved him…"
2 Samuel 12: 23, 34

Despite his great sins, God still called David to his destiny; and a very high calling, it was. David went forward and became a great king. God even described him as "a man after My own heart" and He gave him tremendous favor.

I've heard people say, "But you don't know what I've done. It's unforgiveable." Well, to think so is to minimize, or even negate, the sacrifice made for you on the cross. That's why the cross was so brutal and the Person who died was the greatest of them all – because no greater sacrifice has ever been made, or ever will be made, than the sacrifice God made when He sent His only begotten Son to die for you!

God knows how you were formed. He made you, He placed within you certain gifts, He developed your character, much of it through pain, and He wants to bring all of this together and use it for your good and the good of others.

Only you can do what God made you to do. You may not feel qualified. You may not feel worthy. But God says that you are! Stop keeping yourself from your God-Track by refusing to agree with God about your worthiness. The issue has already been settled. Submit your life and your will to His. He has great plans for you! Remember what we established in the previous chapter: the worse your pain was, the greater your calling going forward is. The more time you spent in failure, the greater your God-Track.

Give Careful Thought:
If your enemy tries to tell you that you're either too good to do what God wants, or you're not good enough; each of these extremes is wrong. He's trying to distract or weaken you from fulfilling your God-Track. Refuse to accept either of these assessments and vow only to receive God's assessment of you.

If you feel unworthy enough to rise up and meet the calling God has on your life, I challenge you to allow Him to turn this attitude around for you. If He has called you to do something specific, it's imperative that you obey Him. Disobeying or delaying your obedience will only compound the problem; possibly leading you into to a valley of blight, or even a blighted life. If you feel unworthy, submit yourself to Him and let Him speak to you and do for you what only He can do.

In addition to understanding this and letting God's view of you sink into your soul, making good decisions in your life will also build your self-esteem. As you continue to ruminate in both things – the way God sees you and the building up of your *self*-esteem – you will get stronger and stronger, no matter what point you're starting from.

Allow yourself to be open to the concept that you are, indeed, worthy of God's calling. Align your path with the one He has for you and get on your God-Track.

20

Do You Believe God is Mean?

The Bible speaks of God's kindness all the way through it. Again, and again, throughout the Old Testament, God tells the Israelites to turn from their idols and worship Him so they'll have peace, stability and prosperity because that's what He wants to give them. That is what He wants to give all of us.

But the Bible is also very "real." In the book of Ruth, for example, Naomi lived through tragic circumstances that just seemed unrelenting. First, her husband died, and over the next ten years both of her sons died as well. This was devastating in the ancient world for several reasons. Not only did she suffer immense emotional grief from those losses, but it also left her financially destitute. Since she was no longer a young woman, her prospects of making a living and/or finding a new husband to support her were little to none. She was left in a state of utter despair and hopelessness. And if all of that weren't enough, she thought she would be leaving her two daughters-in-law and returning to her home town of Bethlehem all alone.

Can you imagine losing literally everyone and everything in your life, only to be forced to return to your hometown in that state of grief and destitution? It would be like attending your high school reunion while you're suffering in poverty and despair, just so your blighted life could be on display to everyone in your community, adding a keen sense of humiliation to your pain?! That's what was about to happen to Naomi.

"But Naomi said, "Return home, my daughters. Why would you come with me? ...¹² Return home, my daughters; I am too old to have another husband. Even if I thought there was still hope for me—even if I had a husband tonight and then gave birth to sons—¹³ would you wait until they grew up? Would you remain unmarried for them? No, my daughters. It is more bitter for me than for you, because the LORD's hand has turned against me!"
Ruth 1: 11-13

Naomi felt as though God had scourged her life and would continue to do so until the day she died. It's no wonder she had developed a belief that God was not kind; at least not to her. I felt this way, myself. I had years in which I felt that God had blighted my life so badly and for so long that I just no longer believed He was kind. At least not to me.

"Don't call me Naomi," she told them. "Call me Mara, because the Almighty has made my life very bitter. ²¹ I went away full, but the LORD has brought me back empty. Why call me Naomi? The LORD has afflicted me; the Almighty has brought misfortune upon me."
Ruth 1:20-21

Naomi means "pleasant;" Mara, the new name Naomi was suggesting for herself, means "bitter."

I had believed that if I had had anything like God's power, I would never have allowed my son to go through so much pain as a child. Although he had a lot of love in his life, he also had traumas that, for a long time, I struggled with forgiving God for allowing. And then there were our business and financial losses

126

that went on and on for so many years, only adding to our bewilderment and pain. What was God thinking?

But we live in a fallen, weary world. And we have to realize that in our human condition we are limited with partial perception (which I refer to as "p.p."). We humans only have eyes in the front of our heads; we aren't omniscient. And our condition of "p.p." is exacerbated by the blindness caused by a plethora of hurts. We just can't see the entire picture; nor can we see truth in its purest form. We aren't capable. And it's because our perspectives are only partial that we sometimes need to exercise faith and trust and submission to God. As I said earlier, faith starts where logic and partial perception leave off.

I'm not talking about reverie or fantasy - placing your blind faith in just anything. I'm talking about placing your faith in The God of Hope, and in the principles and promises of His Word. God is the one thing, the *only* One who has the most well established, proven track record for bringing about goodness in this world. He is the One who can improve, even completely turn around, your life.

So, even though you may not be able to see it now, I urge you to have faith in God's kindness. The Bible says He is kind, and the Bible is *God-breathed;* the only inerrant truth there is. The Bible says God cannot lie. And so, despite that we have experiences which the devil wants to use to skew our beliefs to the contrary, we must have faith and believe in God's goodness. At least be willing while you ask God to show you something good as a sign of His wonderful intentions toward you.

Ruth is the hero of the story because she refuses to go back to her family in her hometown. She sees what Naomi is going through and she's driven by heartfelt compassion for her. Ruth has an epiphany and in one twinkling moment she realizes what her God-Track is. She clings to Naomi, devoting her future to her and even declaring that she will take up faith in Naomi's God.

This act on Ruth's part depicts the moment of her spiritual conversion. In addition to that, the story is symbolic of how sometimes in life we need to have that same dedication to God! No matter what it looks like, no matter how strongly we feel to return to our familiar, comfortable place, we have to forge ahead in faith and unequivocally devote our hearts to Him. This includes having an undying belief in His goodness despite our circumstances "on the ground."

By the end of the book, both Ruth and Naomi have had such a complete turnaround in their circumstances that their hearts are *overflowing* with joy and gratitude.

"He has not stopped showing his kindness to the living and the dead."
Ruth 2:20

Naomi ends up blessed with Ruth, Ruth's wealthy and morally upright husband, Boaz, and also with a grandson. She has her property and her life redeemed. And the women of the town see the miracles God has done in her life as they remind her that God did not leave her empty-handed, after all.

"The women said to Naomi: "Praise be to the LORD, who this day has not left you without a kinsman-redeemer. May he become famous throughout Israel! 15 He will renew your life and sustain you in your old age. For your daughter-in-law, who loves you and who is better to you than seven sons, has given him birth."
16 Then Naomi took the child in her arms and cared for him. 17 The women living there said, "Naomi has a son!" And they named him Obed. He was the father of Jesse, the father of David."
Ruth 4: 14-17

In addition to this major life transformation for Naomi and for Ruth, we can't discount the fact that Ruth's son, Obed, became King David's grandfather. And this direct bloodline led to the eventual birth of Jesus. Naomi and Ruth are listed as ancestors to our Lord and Savior – Jesus Christ, Himself! It becomes crystal clear in later years that, even though Naomi had to go through long-suffering, the end result was something truly miraculous, not only in their lives but in generations to come. In fact, through Ruth's devotion to Naomi and her God, God eventually brought about the greatest of all miracles the world has ever seen: the birth, death, and resurrection of His Son, Jesus Christ.

Give Careful Thought:
Have you fallen prey to believing that God must be mean if He allows all the horrible things that go on in this world? Have you believed that He is responsible for mankind's sickness? Or, that He has personally forgotten you, been mean to you, or just doesn't care about you anymore? Do you feel that He has left you?

Remember that God does everything for a purpose, and when it comes to you He does everything in the absence of malice.

Meditate for a moment on this Scripture:

"As the heavens are higher than the earth,
so are my ways higher than your ways and my thoughts higher
than your thoughts."
Isaiah 55:9

Look through the Attributes of God in the back of this book, especially read the Scriptures under the attribute: "God is Good."

You can also focus on His other attributes such as: "God is Faithful, Just, and Wise."

Does reading through these scriptures give you a renewed perspective about God?

Try praying this prayer:
Lord, please forgive me for my wrong perception of You; sometimes seeing You as a God who is mean. Please redirect my thoughts to be accurate about You, refreshing my belief that You are Who You Are: Love; good and kind; full of grace and mercy; The God of Hope. Thank You, Lord. Amen.

21

Do You Trust God, Completely?

Trust, like hope, is an act that is forward looking. In order to trust someone going forward, you need to have an established track record of past experiences with them. They need to have proven to you that they're trustworthy for you to move ahead with, by way of their past, well-established actions.

Forgiveness is one thing, trust is another. Forgiveness is crucial to you having peace and to finding and keeping your spiritual health. Whenever possible, the Bible says we should seek peace in our relationships with one another. But that doesn't mean that you should offer up your trust to someone indiscriminately. It's important that we distinguish between the two.

This is an area that carries with it a high degree of responsibility toward yourself and others. While it's important to generally trust people and not be obsessed with distrust and paranoia, it's also important that you don't issue trust to someone who hasn't proven themselves to you yet, or has proven to be untrustworthy. That's especially true when the issue or item you would be entrusting to the other person is one of significant value. You wouldn't hand over one of your children to someone unless you know they have a proven track record of accountability; that they are highly responsible, good-hearted and kind, honest, and that they have good judgment. You wouldn't marry someone unless you had a level of comfort that they held these same attributes – responsibility, accountability, loving-kindness, honesty, and possessing good judgment and wisdom.

When you do have well-founded trust in someone it means that you have little-to-no fear in moving forward with that person, too. Their actions thus far have given you a good degree of confidence that everything will be alright with them.

When it comes to trusting God, everything is on the line. Talk about the item being entrusted to the other person being something of great value! We are called to trust God with our very lives and our entire future!

I struggled with a lack of trust in God for years. So many bad things had happened in our lives! How could I trust Him with my future when He had allowed so many tragedies to overwhelm us for so long? How could I have confidence that in my future everything was going to be alright if I entrusted God with everything – with my very life?

I knew the Bible. I knew what some of the prophets and the disciples had to go through to meet their calling. Persecution, humiliation, abuse and even torture. I just didn't believe I was strong enough to withstand these things should God require that I walk through a fire that was hotter than the one I'd already been in for so long. I had struggled greatly with the grief of losing people I'd loved and all the other life-blight the Lord had, in my opinion, purposely put us through. After years in this condition of life-blight, I'd barely held onto any shred of belief in God's goodness, as it was. "I've barely made it this far!" I would say to the Lord.

There is a cost to obtaining any semblance of spiritual maturity. And while I was paying this cost through longsuffering, I was kicking and screaming the whole way. Bless the Lord for His grace and mercy, because we made it through that time of "trial by fire" together, and I and my son came through with our faith intact. In fact, it's now stronger than ever.

Trusting God is also an issue of control. I was terrified of letting go of control of my own life and giving full control to Him. But for me to think I had any control over my life in the first place was nothing but a fallacy, anyway. Believing I possessed the necessary power over my life to do myself any good was an affliction of my "p.p.": partial perception.

The only thing I was controlling was that I was holding myself back with my lack of trust in God. I was paralyzed and stuck in nothing but mire. By staying stuck in that place, I was only adding to my own pain. There, in that pit, I had grief, and piling on top of it was a lack of purpose as I wallowed in the quagmire; only adding to the problem. God-given purpose is like a lifeline; a rope that will pull you out of quicksand. But to be in a position to catch the rope, you have to reach up. You have to trust God!

I realized that in order to rise up to fulfill my God-Track, I had to trust God to guide my path and believe that He wouldn't let my faith fail, no matter what happens in the future. This was a decision; a choice that had to be made.

I had to decide to trust God with everything. If I were to need courage at some time in the future, I had to trust that He would provide it. I had to decide that I would trust Him to provide whatever I needed in order to do whatever He called me to do, whether it be opportunity, wisdom, courage, money, strength, faith….whatever it is; whenever I need it.

Give Careful Thought:
Do you completely trust God with your future? Do you have confidence that, no matter what happens, everything will be alright with Him at the wheel; in complete control of your life?

Meditate on these Scripture verses:

Proverbs 3:5-6
Trust in the LORD with all your heart and lean not on your own understanding; in all your ways submit to Him, and He will make your paths straight.

Haggai 2:4
"Be strong, all you people of the land" declares the LORD, "and work. For I am with you," declares the LORD Almighty.....And my Spirit remains among you. Do not fear."

Ephesians 3:16-21 (NLT)
"I pray that from His glorious, unlimited resources He will empower you with inner strength through His Spirit. [17] Then Christ will make His home in your hearts as you trust in Him. Your roots will grow down into God's love and keep you strong. [18] And may you have the power to understand, as all God's people should, how wide, how long, how high, and how deep His love is. [19] May you experience the love of Christ, though it is too great to understand fully. Then you will be made complete with all the fullness of life and power that comes from God.
[20] Now all glory to God, who is able, through His mighty power at work within us, to accomplish infinitely more than we might ask or think. [21] Glory to Him in the church and in Christ Jesus through all generations forever and ever! Amen."

Also, read some more of the "Attributes of God" in the back of this book. Does this help you to lay your future in God's hands?

If not, what is holding you back? Pray that Jesus will remove any barriers and give you complete trust in Him to give you hope and establish you on your God-Track.

22

Do Not Fear

Haggai 2: 5
"This is what I covenanted with you when you came out of Egypt. And my Spirit remains among you. Do not fear."

Isaiah 54:17
"... no weapon forged against you will prevail, and you will refute every tongue that accuses you."

Fear can be hope's killer, and it can also be a major obstacle to fulfilling your God-Track. At some point in your life you're going to have to deal with fear; whether it be a little or a lot. If you let it, fear will waylay you from your destiny. The devil wants to devour you with fear, and, as I said, it's almost guaranteed that you will have to deal with it sooner or later. Decide now that you won't let fear distract you, set you back, or overwhelm you. Decide here and now that you will refuse to allow fear to have any power over you, with God's help.

In the Bible, God says repeatedly not to fear. Again, and again, He gave the ancient Israelites this command. God made His point with Jonah when He told Jonah to go and warn the people of Nineveh that He was going to destroy the city if the people didn't turn away from their sin, but Jonah was too afraid to do what God called Him to do. Jonah hid from God, or so he foolishly tried. But when Jonah hid on a ship that sailed away from Nineveh and God threw the seas up into an absolute tempest, Jonah realized it was God, and God alone, Who was to be feared. God also told the returning remnant, "Do not fear," in Haggai, because they were directed to rebuild the temple in the presence of their wicked and ruthless enemies who were craving their destruction.

One of the stories which impacted me in my walk with the Lord is a story of how a pastor friend of mine, and his wife, dealt with fear when their six-year-old son was kidnapped and held for ransom. I've included this true story, because it has many lessons in it about dealing with fear when we're faced with a spiritual battle. Jean and his wife, Marcia, have inspired many with this story:

It was Friday, November 29th, 2002, and Pastor Jean Heder of the Famille Tabernacle de Louange Church in Port-au-Prince, Haiti was getting ready to leave for the day. "All aboard!" he yelled out in the church yard to round up his kids to go home. The children had been picked up from school a little earlier by the driver and brought to the church yard where they'd been running around playing, as Pastor Jean finished his work day there. Just like they did every day.

When he came outside, Jean noticed the gate attendant wasn't at his post, but he didn't think much of it. That is, until his youngest son, Matthew, began telling him in his own way, that his brother, Jason, had left in a car with someone. At only two years old, Matthew used sounds and hand gestures more than he used words. He extended his arms and made movements that looked like he was grasping a steering wheel as he said, "He went vroom-vroom, Daddy." Then, he pretended to honk a car horn, "Beep, beep!" he exclaimed. Pastor Jean could also make out that Matthew was upset that his older brother, Jason, had gotten to go for a car ride without him. Despite his age, Matthew was perfectly capable of expressing his displeasure with the unfairness of the situation.

After Jason hadn't turned up from a cursory search of the building and grounds, Pastor Jean called the police. However, the evening only turned into night as they searched every nook and cranny of that church property as well as the surrounding area for Jason, to no avail. As night came over them on that first day of Jason's absence, the reality of their situation sank in. Jason was gone. And he'd apparently left the church grounds with someone in a car, according to Matthew.

Pastor Jean took his wife, Marcia, and their other children home. It was a struggle to keep his head together, but he knew he had to. He asked Marcia if they could enter into a covenant, agreeing that they would not share their feelings with each other, but only scripture, until their ordeal was over. She agreed. There would be not one word of fear or worry, but only the Word of God spoken into this situation, they agreed.

Pastor Jean returned to the church that night. He didn't talk to anyone. He didn't eat…he only prayed. About midnight he heard the Lord say, *"This is not your battle."*

Saturday morning at 9:00 a.m., the first call from the kidnappers came in. "Jean Heder?" the voice at the other end of the line said, rather rudely. "That's *Pastor* Jean Heder," said Jean, correcting him. Never before had he cared how anyone referred to him. Even though he possesses a Doctorate of Divinity Degree, he's never expected to be called "Doctor Heder" by anyone. He's never cared if you referred to him as Pastor or just called him Jean. He's a humble man. But this time, it mattered. Something within him knew he had to make it clear to whomever was behind this evil plot that they were dealing with a man of God. They may not be smart enough to realize it, but *it mattered.* And, God help them, they had laid their hands on a child of God's.

And it worked. Jean immediately felt the attitude and tonality of the kidnapper's voice deflate. Suddenly not so confident, the voice said, "We have your son. We're the police. It's going to cost you 1 million dollars, U.S."

Pastor Jean replied, "If you ask me for 1 million dollars, you must know me. If you've heard me speak about God, you know I'm calling money into my life; that means I don't have it yet." He knew he had to buy some time, although he wasn't sure yet exactly what for. Jean Heder had no idea how to get his son out of this situation; he just knew he had to trust God. Fear was at the door, trying every second to creep into his mind and heart, but he had to fight off the urge to let it enter. The stakes were way too high. If he allowed fear to enter his mind at all, it would surely overtake him. Any amount of fear would only weaken his spiritual power. It could even crush him when his son, his wife, and his family needed him most. In this case, Jean felt that fear could quite literally be a killer.

The kidnappers didn't have any choice but to agree to give him some time to raise the money. One of them, a male, called a couple more times for status updates as the hours of Saturday slowly wore on, and Jean told him each time that he was working on it. After the first phone call Saturday morning and the initial ransom demand had been made, Jean had managed to send out a few emails to key friends and family members briefly telling what had happened, and asking for prayer. The kidnapper had told him not to call the police or he would never again see his son alive, and Jean knew that was a real possibility. Corruption was common in the police force, and he didn't know who he could trust there. If the kidnappers had someone in on their conspiracy who also served on the police force and Jean called the police, the kidnappers could be tipped off that he had disobeyed them.

140

He couldn't risk that. After all, in that first call they had said they *were* the police. In fact, when the first phone call had come in and the man at the other end had said that, the first thought that had struck Jean's mind was, "Oh, good, the police found him. Okay, tell me where I can come and pick him up." But as soon as they'd made that demand for "1 million dollars, U.S.," it was obvious what was happening. It had struck Jean as funny that they'd identified themselves as the police, though. So he heeded the kidnapper's warning and didn't call the police again, other than that initial call to report Jason missing Friday afternoon.

As Jean secluded himself for prayer and fasting, the emails received by Jean's closest friends and allies went "viral," and people from all over began praying for six-year-old Jason, for Jean and Marcia, and for the rest of the family.

In the afternoon on Saturday the kidnappers called again. Jean said, "I have $1,000." The male voice said, "That's not enough to clean my shoes." Pastor Jean replied, "Well, you must have some expensive shoes." He let them know he was working on meeting their demands, but also that their expectations may be a little rich.

Another pastor friend of Jean and Marcia's from the area, told them he had a friend on the police force; someone they could trust. In fact, he commanded his own special victims' unit which specialized in kidnappings. Only with this trusted reference did Jean reach out to him. This police officer advised Jean to be compliant and act very docile with these people, handling them with "kid gloves." But while at the police station talking with the commander, Jean's phone rang again. It was him. The male voice of the kidnapper asked, once again, for an update on the money-raising efforts. Pastor Jean told him he didn't have the money, and since it was Saturday, he probably wouldn't have it until Monday. Then, Jean did something that astounded the commander. After he told the kidnappers he wouldn't have the money until Monday, Jean hung up on them.

The commander, a professional investigator, had never before seen a family member of a kidnapping victim act with such command of the situation; he'd never seen such audacity, without fear. It surprised him so much that it "raised his eyebrows," so to speak. Jean didn't act anything like a victim, which caused the commander to question whether he really was one. For a fleeting moment in time, he wondered if Jean might be involved in his own son's abduction for the purposes of raising money for himself. He even followed Jean back to his home, questioned him, and conducted his own brief investigation. But he soon realized Jean was completely innocent in the matter; he just had an extraordinary quality of strength and confidence, which was difficult for someone without the spiritual power to understand. After Jean had hung up on the evildoers while in the commander's presence, he said to Jean, "You act like *you're* the one in charge." To which Jean replied, "I *am* in charge." In the spirit realm, the pastor knew his position. He had God on his side and in this he was fully confident. He knew the resources that were at his disposal. The spiritual forces of God were far greater than the spiritual forces that were with those kidnappers; in fact, they were greater than anyone could imagine.

Jean and Marcia knew they were in a spiritual battle for their son's life. There was no room for distraction, no room whatsoever for weakness. Jean did not speak to anyone. He didn't want empathy or sympathy from anyone, because these feelings were symptomatic of fear, and he just could *not* afford that.

As Jean continued into that evening in isolation, fasting and praying, he turned off his phone.

Give Careful Thought:

Do you trust God, so much so that you have no fear about your future? If you're facing a difficult challenge in your life, I want you to continue reading to find out how Pastor Jean and his wife, Marcia, held to their belief in the Word of God, even as they were in the battle of a lifetime, surrounded by darkness.

So far in this story, what have Pastor Jean and his wife, Marcia, put into practice I order to disallow fear to enter the picture?

_____

_____

_____

_____

_____

_____

23

The Ambassador

When Sunday morning came, the family went to church, as always. Minus Jason, of course. Jean told the worship leader, "You're off today. I'm going to lead worship." He watched as the place filled beyond capacity. In addition to the church's regular congregation members, people poured in from the surrounding communities. The place was packed, inside and out. Everyone wanted to know how this man of God; the one who preached about faith, was going to act under such bleak circumstances. Would his faith hold up under this kind of pressure? Would he still praise God when his own son's life was in peril?

Ironically, Jean had been doing a series entitled, "The Kingdom of God." In fact, the Sunday prior, he'd taught on 2 Corinthians 5:20, in which Paul says, *"We are therefore Christ's ambassadors, as though God were making his appeal through us."*

This Sunday, as the packed church watched, Pastor Jean opened the service by tearing up a piece of paper that he held up. "I am no longer a "Christian," he said. As eyes widened and backs straightened up a bit, he knew everyone was waiting to see what he was going to say. Was he going to denounce Christ because He hadn't prevented his son from being kidnapped? He could hear more than one person crying, as well-meaning members of his congregation expressed their heartfelt sympathy. He refused to receive it. He had to forge on. "Nowhere in the Bible, am I referred to as a Christian," he said. "As a believer in Jesus Christ, the Bible says that I'm now a citizen of heaven, an Ambassador of God, and even a child of The Most High God; a member of His family. But nowhere does it say that I'm called a Christian."

Pastor Jean had taught his parishioners what it meant to be an Ambassador of God's government. Yes, you're charged with representing Him properly and protecting His interests on the earth. But as an Ambassador you're also entitled to the benefits that your government carries with it. And in God's government, there is mighty power.

"Imagine that you're not only a citizen of the United States, but an Ambassador of the United States' government, and your son were kidnapped," he explained to me later. "Imagine the resources at your disposal. Imagine what would happen to those kidnappers. There would be no safe place on earth for them to hide."

When you think about being "An Ambassador" this way, you realize what he's saying. You would have the full weight and force of the United States government rain down on your enemy's head. What power you would have behind you; what resources – the intelligence community, the military. If such a thing were to happen to you as an Ambassador, God forbid, you would have confidence that the forces behind you were greater than the forces with the wrongdoers, whoever they were. But on this particular Sunday, Pastor Jean taught what the Bible says: There is no greater force in heaven or earth than the power of God. And as an Ambassador of God's government, Jean knew he had the full weight of this power on his side.

He felt inspired to sing a song they sometimes would sing in worship, but *this* time it had special meaning. This time, it was a declaration, intended toward specific evil spirits and specific evil men, in a very specific set of circumstances.

The song went something like this:

"You're wrong to touch a child of God.
You're wrong; you're wrong.
Because Jesus is a lion
and this Lion will devour you.
You're wrong; you're wrong."

The Bible is very clear on this matter. When it comes to the persecution and attacks against Christians - Ambassadors of the government of God, in fact, God's own children – you'd better look out. If you come against a Child of the Most High God, you *will* be destroyed. 1 Corinthians 3:16-17 says: *"Don't you know that you yourselves are God's temple and that God's Spirit dwells in your midst? 17 If anyone destroys God's temple, God will destroy that person; for God's temple is sacred, and you together are that temple."*

Any questions?

The song rang out as the congregation and all the visitors joined in.

"...Jesus is a lion and this Lion will devour you."

When the service was over and all the people had left, Pastor Jean finally turned his phone back on. It rang almost immediately.

"Looks like you don't want the merchandise. So, we're gonna flush it" the male voice said. Clearly, not being able to call whenever he'd wanted to; not being able to get Pastor Jean to jump through hoops at his whim had irritated him.

"Make that the last time you refer to my son as "the merchandise"! I don't want to talk to you again until I talk to my son!" And with that, Pastor Jean hung up on his son's kidnappers, once again.

About an hour later, the phone rang again. Jean recognized the number. They'd been calling him from several different numbers, and he had been logging every call in a notebook with the date, time, and number present on the caller ID. This time on the other end of the line, it was his beloved son, Jason. "Hi Daddy," he said. "Jason, how are you?" his father asked. "I am blessed, Daddy," he replied with what he'd been well-taught to say. "They lied to me, Daddy," the six-year-old explained. "First, they said they'd take me home and they didn't. Then, I told them I have to go to church. They said they would take me. But did you see, Daddy, I wasn't at church today?" Jean had to maintain his composure. "Now, they're telling me they'll take me to my birthday party next week, but I can't believe them, since they already lied about the other things!"

Jean, the man of God, said this to his son, "Jason, remember Philippians 4:13, "I can do all things through Christ, Who strengthens me. You're a winner, man!" Then, he went on, "Jason, I've never lied to you. Ever. And I'm telling you – tomorrow night you will sleep in your own bed and you will eat at my table." At that moment, the kidnappers took the phone from him, which infuriated Jean because he wanted the precious boy to speak to his mother, Marcia. Jean screamed at them, "Give him the phone!!" And they complied. The phone went back to little Jason so he could hear his mother's comforting voice. When they were finished, the male voice came back on the phone and Jean told him, "If you touch my son, your whole family will be in trouble."

Then, for the third night in a row, Jean went into seclusion. And once again, he turned off his phone.

When Jean had discovered his son was missing on Friday afternoon, he had determined he would not eat again until his son was home. And so, now going into the third night of this epic spiritual battle, with his son's life on the line, he still did not eat.

First thing Monday morning, Jean turned his phone back on and the kidnappers called right away. He explained that he was out and about looking for money. The kidnappers told Jean they were out of phone cards, and asked him to buy them some time for their phones. "You're *what*?" he said. At first, he thought, "Well, I'm not going to help them in their evil endeavors." But then he realized their request was just another display of weakness for them. Also, he needed them to stay in communication with him, so he bought them two $20.00 phone cards. When he gave them the first set of numbers, he told them when that card was finished he'd give them the other one.

Jean called the police commander and asked him if he could look up the 3 main phone numbers the kidnappers had been calling him from, which he'd been recording in his notebook. They identified them right away. "Can you please send some undercover officers over here?" Jean asked the commander. He didn't know what they would do, but he knew the end of this ordeal was drawing near; he could somehow feel it.

Jean called Marcia, and together, as they had promised one another, they prayed the Scriptures. They declared Matthew 18:19, in which Jesus Himself said, "*Again, truly I tell you that if two of you on earth agree about anything they ask for, it will be done for them by my Father in heaven.*" Jean and Marcia were sure that never before had two individuals prayed with more conviction; and with both of their interests in complete alignment with one another. They wanted their son returned home unharmed. And they wanted him home now.

The declaration of this Scripture, and their subsequent prayers for their son, carried power, and they knew it. They prayed that the Lord would insulate Jason from any harmful effects of this experience, just as an electrical wire is fully encapsulated in its plastic insulation. In prayer, Jean demanded that the kidnappers call from one of the numbers he knew the police were tracking. "I demand they call me from the number 555-1211!" He didn't know why he chose that number, but he did.

About 11 o'clock in the morning, only one hour after he'd asked for undercover police officers to come to his home, Pastor Jean received a call from the Commander. "We have men in position now. What's your plan?" he asked Jean. Jean didn't have a plan! But he knew God did. He and Marcia made arrangements that the next time the kidnappers called, he would wave as a signal to Marcia, and she would call the Commander and tell him they're on the phone and which number they were using. Since they're tracking the locations of the phones, they should be able to close in on them. About 3:00 o'clock Monday afternoon, the call came in, and it came from the phone number 555-1211, just as Jean had commanded in his prayers! When Jean recognized the number on his phone, he waved at Marcia before he even answered it. He knew he needed to keep the wicked man at the other end on the line for as long as possible, in order for the tracking to work and the police to be able to get to it in time. Jean knew his phone would roll over to voicemail on the sixth ring, so he let it ring five times, and then answered it quickly. The man at the other end was not happy at all that he'd had to wait to have his call answered. When he expressed his displeasure at his inconvenience, Jean just began to rant, "You are the one making me run all over the place looking for money! You are the one who has my son! What do you expect? I'm working on meeting your demands. In fact, I've found someone who is willing to give

150

me $500,000!.....," he went on and on, continuing to spout off to the man for a period of four entire minutes while he ran up and down the stairs. He doesn't remember everything he said, he just knew he couldn't give them any opportunity to hang up the phone or get off that line. He had to string him along long enough to give the commander and his men time to find them and close in, so he couldn't let the guy get a word in edgewise.

After his four minute rant, he heard nothing at the other end....then he heard the phone hit the wall. He kept saying, "Hello! Do you understand? Hello?"

Seven full minutes after the call had begun, and 3 minutes after he'd quit speaking and heard the phone hit the wall, someone hung up the receiver and the line went dead.

Believe

Jean and Marcia didn't know what had happened. They didn't know if the police had found the kidnappers, or if Jason was rescued or safe. But what they did know was the Biblical principal of declaring with faith, as Jesus said to do in Mark 11:24: *"Therefore I tell you, whatever you ask for in prayer, believe that you have received it, and it will be yours."* They began declaring out loud in their house, "We found him! We have him! Yay! We have him!" Their help said, "Where is he? You have him? Is he back?" to which Jean had to explain, "We don't know where or how he'll be returned yet, but we declare that he is safe now and we have him. We believe."

Fear was still trying to get in the door and take hold. So they kept declaring, they kept worshipping, and they kept praying. As he had done all weekend, the man of God kept praying:
2 Corinthians 10:5: *"We demolish arguments and every pretension that sets itself up against the knowledge of God, and we take captive every thought to make it obedient to Christ."*

Four o'clock came and went. Then five o'clock. They kept declaring, kept worshipping, kept praying.

Finally, at six p.m., Pastor Jean Heder received the call they'd been waiting for from the police commander. They had apprehended the kidnappers, rescued Jason, and he was safe. When he told Marcia, she finally broke down. She was sobbing so hard, she could hardly stand up and go with Jean to the station to retrieve their beloved son.

It turned out that when the kidnappers used that phone, the one Jean demanded they use while in prayer, it was located inside a public phone booth. The police tracked its location and while Jean had been going on and on in his four-minute rant, the police had had enough time to close in on him. When they arrived at the phone booth they apprehended the kidnapper. They got him to take them to the place where they were holding their victims. One of the other kidnappers was there and was arrested. Also, in addition to having kidnapped little Jason, they'd abducted another victim - a woman. Both victims were safely rescued. The woman who had been held with Jason told police that Jason had given his captors a hard time. He wasn't easy, docile, or compliant, she explained. He had refused to drink tap water, requiring their captors to go to the store and buy him bottled water. He wouldn't eat certain foods, and insisted on having other things from the store.

Jason told his father later that when the man came to take him out of the church yard that fateful Friday, he had put his hand over Jason's mouth and threatened to kill him if he screamed.

Now that Jason is grown up, Pastor Jean says he can tell the story and laugh. It's had no ill effects on him whatsoever. If anything, the experience strengthened his faith in God's goodness and His power.

In all other cases of kidnappings, the Heder's have heard of in Haiti, none of the victims have survived except Jason and the woman he was held captive with. Of the three known kidnappers, all three are now dead. The two that were caught died in jail. And the word on the street was that the other one, who was not apprehended at the time of the rescue but was known to police, ended up being killed by the police sometime later. He'd never been caught, but he lived in constant fear. One day he was walking down the street and began to get paranoid simply because a police car was behind them. The police didn't know who he was, but he panicked. The street he was walking down was a dead end, giving him nowhere to turn; nowhere to run. In his dread and hysteria, he turned around and pulled out a gun, so the police shot him to death.

"You're wrong to touch a child of God.
You're wrong. You're wrong.
Because Jesus is a lion
and this Lion will devour you.
You're wrong. You're wrong."

Give Careful Thought:
Do you have fear about moving forward which is depleting your hope for a bright future? What lessons did you learn by reading the story of Pastor Jean's son's kidnapping, and how The Ambassador of God's Government handled the situation?

The Word of God is true, whether you see it or not. You can be experiencing a tremendous storm – even a hurricane – but the sun still exists and it still shines. Just because you can't see it, doesn't mean it's not there. The Word of God tells us that we're not to fear. Once you become a Christian, you can avail yourself of the power of the God-of-the-Angel-Armies because you are His child; an Ambassador of His government.

Meditate of these Scripture verses:

Psalm 84:11
"For the LORD God is a sun and shield;
the LORD bestows favor and honor;
no good thing does he withhold
from those whose walk is blameless."

Psalm 56:3 (NKJV)
"Whenever I am afraid, I will trust in You."

Fear can be so debilitating and can rob you of your hope, so I want you to take steps to eliminate it from your life right now. You'll need to continue to refuse to allow it into your life daily, but this is possible for you to do because with God *all things* are possible. Keep focusing on the Bible, and what it says about fear. Keep your focus on Jesus.

Based on the principles put into practice by Pastor Jean Heder and his wife, Marcia, when their son was kidnapped, here are some things you may do to fight off fear if you're entering a life-storm or fear-provoking ordeal: In fact, practicing these principles can help you if you have a general sense of fear about your future:

- Refuse to speak about your feelings of fear or sadness.
- Speak only faith-building, life-giving Scriptures into the situation (i.e.: Philippians 4:13, "I can do all things through Christ, Who strengthens me.")

- Find another person – someone who has a greatly vested interest in the situation – and enter into a covenant with one another that you will do the above 2 steps together.
- Fast something each day, even if it is potato chips or an apple (something you would have otherwise eaten, had you not been fasting).
- Worship God (there are many praise and worship Scriptures in the Psalms) and pray continuously; especially Scripture verses that are pertinent to overcoming fear and being victorious.
- Realize the battle is God's; not yours.
- Believe in faith that God can bring you through victoriously.

Pray this prayer:
Dear Lord Jesus, I ask You to remove fear from my heart, giving me a renewed sense of strength, confidence, and hopefulness about my future. I take every thought captive to be obedient to Christ (2 Corinthians 10:5). I refuse to allow weakness into my situation – I have God here. I refuse to allow fear to creep into my mind. Be my sun and shield, Lord. Thank You, Jesus. Amen.

How can I be an Ambassador of Christ on this earth? How can I better move forward without fear of the future? Lord, please show me.

24

Be Strong and Courageous

Haggai 2: 4-5

"'But now be strong...' declares the LORD. 'Be strong, ... Be strong, all you people of the land,' declares the LORD, 'and work. For I am with you,' declares the LORD Almighty.... And my Spirit remains among you. Do not fear.'"

Joshua 1: 3, 5-6, 7, 9

³ "I will give you every place where you set your foot, as I promised Moses."

⁵ "No one will be able to stand against you all the days of your life. As I was with Moses, so I will be with you; I will never leave you nor forsake you. ⁶ Be strong and courageous, because you will lead these people to inherit the land I swore to their ancestors to give them."

⁷ "Be strong and very courageous."

⁹ "Have I not commanded you? Be strong and courageous. Do not be afraid; do not be discouraged, for the LORD your God will be with you wherever you go."

When I'm feeling weak or fearful and know I need more strength, I often read Haggai Chapter 2 and Joshua Chapter 1 for inspiration and courage. But there's one character of the Bible to whom I can relate the most; Gideon. Every time I read about him, I laugh out loud. I can't help it; I think of him as sort of a whiner. Gideon believed he had no power whatsoever to change his circumstances or do anything for his people. But God had other plans, and when God has plans for you, *which He does*, you can believe great things are going to happen!

Gideon turns out to be a hero in the end; his story is one of the greatest stories of someone who is pathetically weak; someone who doesn't trust God and who has plenty of self-admitted fear; but still rises up to fulfill his God-Track. Talk about a turnaround!

In Judges, Chapter 6, God hears the cries of the Israelites, who have been subject to the ruthless cruelties of the Midianites for seven years. God sent an angel to earth, and parked him right in Gideon's front yard. And Gideon does what I probably would've done. The angel tries to tell Gideon that God is with him, that He's heard the cries of the people, and He's about to rescue them. But before the angel can get very far, Gideon questions God. After all, his prior experience is contrary to what the angel is telling him, making what the Lord is saying difficult for Gideon to grasp.

"Gideon son of Joash was threshing wheat at the bottom of a winepress to hide the grain from the Midianites. ¹² The angel of the LORD appeared to him and said, 'Mighty hero, the LORD is with you!'
¹³ 'Sir,' Gideon replied, 'if the LORD is with us, why has all this happened to us? And where are all the miracles our ancestors told us about? Didn't they say, The LORD brought us up out of

Egypt? But now the LORD *has abandoned us and handed us over to the Midianites.'"* **Judges 6:11-13**

Gideon was obviously downtrodden and discouraged, and had been for a long time. I've been there. He was hopeless, fearful, and felt powerless. So, imagine his astonishment when God tells him that *he* will be the one who will lead the charge and rescue Israel from the ruthless oppression of their enemy, the Midianites. God had already eluded to what He was about to say when He called Gideon "mighty hero."

"The LORD *turned to him and said, 'Go in the strength you have and save Israel out of Midian's hand. Am I not sending you?'* [15] *'Pardon me, my lord,' Gideon replied, 'but how can I save Israel? My clan is the weakest in Manasseh, and I am the least in my family.'"*
Judges 6:14-15

It's as if Gideon is saying, "Hmmm-hmmm! Objection, Your Honor! You can't possibly mean *me*! That *I* will rescue Israel? Ha! You must've made some mistake, God."

Gideon goes on to ask God for a sign, and the LORD gives him one. Then, still insecure about his God-Track, Gideon asks for *another* sign. And in His grace, the LORD gives it to him again. *Finally*, Gideon buys into God's plan.

He gathered together an army of men, and went out and camped just south of their enemies, ready to wage battle. But God told Gideon he had to downsize his army, dramatically! Once God was finished delivering Israel, He didn't want them to be able to boast that they'd defeated the Midianites in their own power. God knew them; they were prideful and had been missing the mark, in terms of whom they'd been placing their faith in, for a long time.

159

God makes Gideon send over twenty-two thousand soldiers home, instructing him to move forward with only three hundred men.

I love what God did next:

"Now the camp of Midian lay below him in the valley. ⁹ During that night the LORD said to Gideon, 'Get up, go down against the camp, because I am going to give it into your hands.'"
Judges 7: 8-22

But God knows Gideon is afraid, so He gives him a little extra way to build his confidence before he attacks the enemy:
¹⁰ If you are afraid to attack, go down to the camp with your servant Purah ¹¹ and listen to what they are saying. Afterward, you will be encouraged to attack the camp." So he and Purah his servant went down to the outposts of the camp. ¹² The Midianites, the Amalekites and all the other eastern peoples had settled in the valley, thick as locusts. Their camels could no more be counted than the sand on the seashore.
¹³ Gideon arrived just as a man was telling a friend his dream. "I had a dream," he was saying. "A round loaf of barley bread came tumbling into the Midianite camp. It struck the tent with such force that the tent overturned and collapsed."
¹⁴ His friend responded, "This can be nothing other than the sword of Gideon son of Joash, the Israelite. God has given the Midianites and the whole camp into his hands."
Judges 7: 10-14

Next, God provides the victory for Gideon and his men. In one fell swoop God gave Gideon a boost of confidence and strength at the same time that He executed His judgment on the

Midianites causing them confusion and panic. The battle was already won before it started:

15 When Gideon heard the dream and its interpretation, he bowed down and worshiped. He returned to the camp of Israel and called out, "Get up! The LORD has given the Midianite camp into your hands." 16 Dividing the three hundred men into three companies, he placed trumpets and empty jars in the hands of all of them, with torches inside.
17 "Watch me," he told them. "Follow my lead. When I get to the edge of the camp, do exactly as I do. 18 When I and all who are with me blow our trumpets, then from all around the camp blow yours and shout, 'For the LORD and for Gideon.'"
19 Gideon and the hundred men with him reached the edge of the camp at the beginning of the middle watch, just after they had changed the guard. They blew their trumpets and broke the jars that were in their hands. 20 The three companies blew the trumpets and smashed the jars. Grasping the torches in their left hands and holding in their right hands the trumpets they were to blow, they shouted, "A sword for the LORD and for Gideon!" 21 While each man held his position around the camp, all the Midianites ran, crying out as they fled.
22 When the three hundred trumpets sounded, the LORD caused the men throughout the camp to turn on each other with their swords"
Judges 7: 15 - 22

Before Gideon and his men had reached their enemy's camp, the defeat had been secured. Their enemies turned on each other with their swords. The biggest role Gideon's small army played in the entire episode was, quite frankly, to gather up the plunder of their enemies once they had fled in terror.

161

God chose Gideon because he *was* weak. In his weakness God could display His mighty power. But Gideon's fear and his whiney attitude only endeared him to me. It made him very relatable, because I've done the same thing. In fact, I did almost the *exact* same thing when God showed me what my God-Track was. The first thing I did was to remind the Lord about the blight my family members and I had been experiencing for so long, in case He wasn't aware: "If You are there, why have all these bad things happened to us? I thought You were the God Who did great and mighty things, like you did for the Israelites when you parted the Red Sea. Like you used to do for us when we first believed. But those days are long gone. What happened? Where did You go?"

Then, when God showed me the specific calling He had on my life – which was to write a book - I just couldn't believe it. "You want me to do *what*? Write a book? But I don't have any formal education in writing! I have no master's degree in writing; in fact, *no* degree in writing whatsoever! And I don't know anyone in the publishing industry! I completely lack a platform from which to launch a book. So, you must be kidding, right?" That's what I said to God, in a nutshell. Much like Gideon, I pointed out to God all the reasons I was sure He couldn't have meant *me*.

However, God also chose Gideon because He had faith that Gideon would obey Him. And I knew I had to do the same thing. Sometimes, your willingness to serve and obey God is what He needs most, along with the gifts He's already given you, in order to accomplish great and mighty things. There's a reason the story of Gideon is in the Bible! It's because we need to see examples of others who went from the lowest, weakest position to winning an epic battle and freeing a nation! Because that's how God works in our own lives, too.

We need to see that the battle is not ours; just like the Lord told Pastor Jean Heder when his son was kidnapped. The battle did not belong to Gideon. Yes, God used him to accomplish what He had already decided to do, and that made Gideon's role vital. However, we often believe too much of the control over the outcome lies with us and our physical abilities and power (or lack thereof) in the natural realm, when it just doesn't. Whether we think too highly or too lowly of ourselves; either way, we're thinking too much about ourselves!

Let your battle rest on God's shoulders. He's much better equipped to handle it than you are.

Follow His directions, and you'll find your way out in great victory.

Give Careful Thought:
If you have fear, hopelessness, or are facing a daunting challenge that makes you feel overwhelmed, remember Gideon. Remember also the returning remnant at Haggai's time, and how much fear they had of their enemies. But more importantly, remember what God has said: *"Do not fear." "Be strong and courageous." "I am with you."*

Meditate on this Scripture:
"So he said to me, 'This is the word of the LORD to Zerubbabel: Not by might nor by power, but by my Spirit, says the LORD Almighty.'"
Zechariah 4:6

Pray this prayer:
Lord Jesus, please let me know that you're with me and the battle is Yours to wage, not mine. Let the burden of my challenge rest upon Your shoulders, exchanging my heavy yoke for Your light

one. Give me Your strength and hope, making me strong and courageous. Show me my God-Track and give me everything I need to fulfill it. Amen.

"For my yoke is easy and my burden is light."
Matthew 11:30

25

He Knows How You Are Formed

Psalm 103:10-14

"He does not treat us as our sins deserve
  or repay us according to our iniquities.
[11] For as high as the heavens are above the earth,
  so great is His love for those who fear Him;
[12] as far as the east is from the west,
  so far has He removed our transgressions
  from us.
[13] As a father has compassion on his children,
  So the LORD has compassion on those who
  fear Him;
[14] for He knows how we are formed,
  He remembers that we are dust."

When it comes time to get on your God-Track and begin your work for God, one thing you must learn to do is to get "un-bound" from your past mistakes and sins. You just can't let them continue to deter you. God has forgiven them; now it's time for you to do the same and move on.

Of course, you should take responsibility for yourself and your behaviors. Take responsibility for the things that contributed to your walking into the valley where you find yourself. The sooner after the mistake is made that you take responsibility, the sooner God will begin to repair damages for you.

Having done that, realize there comes a point at which it's time to move forward. You've craved improvement, growth, and a greater and better life. Those desires were placed in you by God. God has big plans for your life. He's looking for you to realize that so He can begin to move you onto your God-Track.

Even in the tiny book of Haggai, God speaks to this issue. God speaks to the people of this ancient Jewish culture, in old world language, telling them that, yes, they're defiled with sin, but He still has plans to bless them anyway!

Haggai 2:14, 18-19

"Then Haggai said, 'So it is with this people and this nation in my sight,' declares the LORD. 'Whatever they do and whatever they offer there is defiled.'"
"'From this day on, from this twenty-fourth day of the ninth month, give careful thought to the day when the foundation of the LORD's temple was laid. Give careful thought: [19] Is there yet any seed left in the barn? Until now, the vine and the fig tree, the pomegranate and the olive tree have not borne fruit.
From this day on I will bless you.'"

God does not treat us as our sins deserve. Not matter what you did, no matter how guilty you may feel, or how unworthy, weak, or powerless you may think you are, you have a great destiny! That's what your God-Track is – something big, something great!

As high as the heavens are above the earth – so great is His love *for you*!

As far as the east is from the west, so far has He removed your transgressions *from you*. The past is the only thing in your life that's dead.

He has compassion for you. No one knows better than He does how you were formed, what your mistakes have been, and what you struggle with.

I'm going to say it again: If you think your circumstances are too dire, you're too lowly, or you're not worthy to fulfill God's calling on your life, then you're thinking too much about yourself. You're wrongly thinking that *way* too much power lies in your hands. And *that* can become your greatest actual weakness. Don't get so caught up in your dead past, prior mistakes, or even your overwhelming situation to the point that you get stuck there and miss fulfilling your God-Track.

Take note: once God has shown you what He wants you to do on your God-Track, it's your job to become good at it. Do the best you can to cultivate knowledge, learn everything you can about your particular calling, refine and polish your skills, and master your craft for the benefit of others. And remember to pray and ask God for His help.

Give Careful Thought:
Pray this prayer:
Lord Jesus, please help me move up and out of the valley of guilt or low self-esteem and rise to meet the call of my God-Track, which is of the highest importance.

Lord, help me be free from the mistakes I've made in the past, any and all guilt that I've been carrying around, and any lack of worthiness that I've come to believe about myself. Please show me what You have planned and purposed for me to do. I submit my will to Yours, Lord. I am willing to be used by You and fulfill my God-Track. Please allow me the privilege of serving You, Lord.

Thank You, Lord.

26

What Have You Been Hoping For?

Luke 17:33 (NLT)
"If you cling to your life, you will lose it, and if you let your life go, you will save it."

As Christians, we can tend to "hang our hat" on Scriptures that promise us comfort, prosperity, healing and other "good things." As I said, I call that the "Rosy Gospel." More comfort; that's what we all want so we pull out the Scripture verses that promise those things and forget the rest.

It's fine to hope for more money, better health, and more comfort. Of course, having new opportunities at work or in life can be a great motivator and encourager for us – these things build our hope. But if we're hoping for anything in the natural more than we're hoping for more of God's presence, more opportunities to serve God, or even for Jesus to come back, then our "hope priorities" are in the wrong order.

In fact, if we're hoping for anything on earth more than we're hoping to make it to our eternal home, as one of God's children, we're setting our sights too low. Believe me, if you suddenly came into a fortune in money, changing your life to one of ease, it still would never compare to the life you're headed for when you get to heaven.

As we've established, your character is everlasting and priceless to God and its development is one of His highest priorities. He can use it to work wonders in this world; to rescue others. And when it comes to your faith, if you believe in the things God has said to mankind; if you believe that He sent His Son to rescue you from hell and eternal darkness by way of your faith in Jesus; if you hold God, His Son, and His Holy Spirit in the highest esteem; that is precious to God!

But ask yourself this: If you had had nothing but ease and comfort, would you be as interested in God; seeking Him and His answers for your life? Or would you have become complacent in your life of convenience and pleasure, lacking purpose? For many of us, the answer is obvious; we just weren't asking the right questions until now.

God has been developing and refining your character and your faith so that He can use you to fulfill your End-Time-God-Track. If you didn't have those qualities, you wouldn't be as useful to Him as you are *with* those qualities.

If you didn't have faith in Jesus Christ, you would be securing your own dark destiny. Being on a path toward hell would truly be something to fear and be hopeless about. But you're not on that path; you're on a path toward heaven; a path directed by the very hand of God Himself; a path filled with meaning and purpose. Here, there is good reason to find your courage. Here, there is good reason to have hope.

"'In this place (inside your heart) I will grant peace,' declares the LORD Almighty."
Haggai 2:9

This world can be a dark, devastating place. This is a world in which evil exists, and that fact is to our extreme detriment. All of nature, including the lives of all animals, has been devastated by evil, too. Evil is the cause of all disease, all droughts, blight and lack, all unrest and violence, all depression and mental illness, all suicides, and yes, all hopelessness.

When God created Adam and Eve in the Garden of Eden, it was never His intention that they, and the rest of mankind behind them, would fall into an evil world. But by deceiving them satan achieved his greatest victory. God had given dominion of the earth to Adam and Eve, and they gave it away to satan. (Genesis Chapters 1 through 3). And the rest is one big, horrid line of history. Wars, earthquakes, floods, pestilence, and death have ravaged the earth all throughout mankind's existence.

But the Bible also tells us that satan's rule over this world is limited and restricted, and that it *will* end.

The Bible is the only un-erred, truthful word of God that He gave to humans so we could understand Him. (2 Timothy 3:16). It is through the Bible that we know who He is and what He thinks of us in our less-than-stellar state. And there's a reason it's called "The Good News." Even though many of us wish we were living on a cruise ship and are devastated when we find out we're living on a battleship, the Bible tells us not only that the battle will end, but *how* it will end. We win. That's the "Good News" part – the ending is always hopeful. The ending is victorious, full of peace, health, overwhelming love and bliss.

The only catch is: to share in the blessings coming from God, you have to make a choice.

Heaven and hell are *real* places. Even Christians sometimes forget this. You may have been taught otherwise or you may want to believe otherwise. But God's Truth *is* absolute. I once met a Christian, raised in a Catholic family, who shared with me that she doesn't believe that that hell exists as its own separate place. I pointed out to her Luke 16 –the story of the Rich Man and Lazarus and suggested that she read it. But, just like the rich man in the story who begs Abraham to send Lazarus to his father's house to warn his brothers about hell so they'll repent and avoid that place of torment, you can't convince someone who doesn't want to be convinced. Abraham replied to the rich man, now in the agony of hell, *"If they do not listen to Moses and the Prophets, they will not be convinced even if someone rises from the dead."* (Luke 16:31). God has given us His words, and we're faced with choosing to either believe Him or not.

Just as you can't make up whether or not hell exists, you also cannot make up your own way to heaven. In the Bible, Jesus said, *"No one comes to the Father, except through me."* (John 14:6) You either believe God or you don't. You have free will and you need to exercise it in regard to your beliefs about God.

While it's crucial to each of us that we understand the truth about God, receive Him and have faith in Him, faith is getting harder and harder to have in this world. The Bible says the world will get darker and darker as the days draw closer to Jesus' return, and that's exactly what's happening. I'm fairly confident that you've noticed. If you'd been living a fulfilled, happy life of ease, you probably wouldn't have bought this book.

Although Haggai was written to the returning remnant in 520 B.C., it is an End-Time book as well. Haggai 2:6 God speaks of the return of His Son:

Haggai 2: 6-7
"This is what the LORD Almighty says: 'In a little while I will once more shake the heavens and the earth, the sea and the dry land. I will shake all nations, and The Desired of All Nations (that is, Jesus Christ) will come, and I will fill this house with glory,' says the LORD Almighty."

The house that God is referring to is the modern-day temple, which is the global body of believers or the worldwide church. We know this because the Bible tells us so. Once again, here is 1 Corinthians 3:16:

1 Corinthians 3:16-17

"Don't you know that you yourselves are God's temple and that God's Spirit dwells in your midst? If anyone destroys God's temple, God will destroy that person; for God's temple is sacred, and you together are that temple."

...and He's going to fill "this house" with glory when He returns. Doesn't that sound good? *Glory means hope.* It means grandeur, greatness, honor, splendor, triumph. There's nothing bad in it, at all.

So, what do you hope for? Has your hope been strictly, or even mostly, set on things in this world? For parents who have lost a child, many say it is no longer their highest priority to stay here without their child. They long to go to heaven and be reunited with them. For those of us who have lost parents or other loved ones, we have that same longing.

For many years I was guilty of materialism and selfishness, much like the ancient Israelites at Haggai's time. The only thing I wanted out of life was prosperity and success. I wanted to live on a cruise ship, not a battle ship. I thought material gain would bring "glory" to my life in the way of honor, respect, dignity, and favor, not to mention the added benefits or "perks" that come with having money; an easier, more comfortable life.

However, as I explained in Chapter 13, the Lord put up obstacle after obstacle in my path, and prevented me from having those longings fulfilled. One reason for this was that I was working the wrong land – on the wrong track for my life instead of the one God had ordained for me to be on.

But I'm convinced there's been another reason for all the heartbreak that so many people have been experiencing, including my family members and I. I believe God's purpose in allowing so much devastation to occur on the earth as of late is because He's trying to get us to loosen our grip on this world. God works on the unseen – in our minds and hearts. And He doesn't want us to be too comfortable or attached to this world because He's about to move! He is warning us that He's coming back soon.

I am of the complete and total belief that Jesus is returning sooner than most people realize, and He will reclaim those who belong to Him. Will that include you? Will you be smart and not only put your faith in Him as the Son of God and the one and only way to heaven, but will you be diligently watching, waiting for His imminent return?

Don't let yourself get so distracted by the things of this world that you "miss the boat," for there will be those who do.

In Matthew Chapter 25 Jesus gave the parable of the Ten Virgins and this is exactly what this parable is about. There will be Christians left out at the time of the rapture (The rapture is described in 1 Thessalonians 4:14-17). Remember Lot's wife who turned into a pillar of salt because she looked back. Her heart was not looking toward the angels leading them out of God's devastating wrath; her heart was not fixed on God. Her heart was set on sin, materialism, and the hedonistic pleasures of the life she'd had. That's why she wasn't delivered out of the fire that burned down!

It's alright to hope for things in the natural: a promotion at work, or that the baby you're expecting will be born healthy and have a happy childhood. It's even okay to hope for a new car, home, or other material gain. Hoping for a good future is what this book is all about. But, we tend to see things so temporally;

174

fixing our hopes on the things of this earth as our highest priority. And that's where we can go wrong.

Heaven is a place that is so much better than here on earth in this age, we can scarcely imagine it. So, why would we hope for anything else more than we hope for that? Our hope is best placed when it's fixed on God. Our hope, when fixed on God, cannot be shaken, and our happiness will be less dependent on our circumstances. We know we end in victory as long as we keep watching for Jesus and keep our
faith. We know we end in greater glory, with the greatest gain that will ever be recorded in human history: The exponential gain His people will experience when we're reunited with Him (and all our loved ones who've passed on before us).

Fix your heart and your primary hopes on God. Fix your eyes on Jesus Christ, and hope for His return more than you hope for anything else.

Give Careful Thought:
If your hopes for...

_____

_____

_____

_____

...in your life had been fulfilled and you had had more comforts, more money, and less hardship, would you be looking up, hoping for Jesus to return, or hoping to go to heaven, as much as you are now? Or would your hopes be wrongly placed, fixated on the things of this world?

Is it possible that by denying you an easier life here, God was actually helping you by instilling in you a deeper desire for His return and for your eternal life with Him to begin?

Give Careful Thought:
Pray and ask the Lord Jesus to set your priorities straight, so that you desire Him and His return more than anything else in this world.

27

Right Priorities

Look Up!

Luke 24: 5-6
"Why do you look for the living among the dead?
He is not here; He has risen!"

There are many Christians who were enthusiastic about following Jesus when they first came to believe in Him. Some people, like me, upon discovering the spiritual elation that comes when in His presence, became utterly infatuated with Him. But then, the refining fire came and began to bring with it, difficult circumstances; (the number-one way of developing deeper, better moral character and goodness in a person). This refining process, which comes through difficulty, either draws His followers closer to Him or causes them to move away from Him.

Through Haggai, God came right out and told the Jews that their priorities were wrong:

"This is what the LORD Almighty says: 'These people say, 'The time has not yet come for the LORD'S house to be built.'
Then the word of the LORD came through the prophet Haggai: 'Is it time for you yourselves to be living in your paneled houses, while this house remains a ruin?'"
Haggai 1: 2-4

Jesus also warned His followers in Revelation Chapter 3 about falling asleep, becoming indifferent toward Him, and allowing their love for Him and others to grow cold.

If your spirit has become disenchanted with or indifferent toward God (lukewarm) due to so many bad things happening to you; because of busy-ness or stress; or even if you've become angry with God (cold)…it's time to wake up!

"Yet I hold this against you: You have forsaken your First Love. Remember the height from which you have fallen! Repent and do the things you did at first."
Revelation 2: 4-5

"Wake up! Strengthen what remains and is about to die, for I have not found your deeds complete in the sight of my God. Remember, therefore, what you have received and heard; obey it, and repent. But if you do not wake up, I will come like a thief, and

you will not know at what time I will come to you." **Revelation 3: 2-3**

As I've said previously, when I first came to a belief in Jesus, I couldn't believe the spiritual euphoria I would experience almost every night while reading my Bible and spending time in prayer with the Lord. I became addicted to that feeling. It was all I ever wanted – to be in the presence of Jesus as often as possible. If you've experienced it, you know what I'm talking about. But if you haven't experienced the spiritual ecstasy that *is* Jesus Christ, you don't know what you are missing! There's not one thing in this world that can even come close to that feeling – no drug or alcoholic beverage or any amount of either one, no sexual experience, no euphoric experience of human love or being "in love" that compares to the overwhelming feeling of love, peace, and elation that *is* the presence of the Lord.

"Were not our hearts burning within us while He talked with us on the road (to Emmaus) and opened the Scriptures to us?" **Luke 24:32**

Each night, I would put my young son to bed around 9 o'clock. I would then go into worship and prayer alone in my bedroom, invariably ending up in an overwhelming state of utter spiritual bliss. I would cry – every time. In fact, I'd often sob until I would ask the Lord to pull away from me because of the headache that always came from sobbing so hard for so long; then I would feel Him retreat. Of course, I could sense that His power was so immense; I'd never be able to survive being in His full presence in my natural state – in this body.
The presence of the Holy Spirit is that intense and Jesus reaches the deepest areas of your soul.

God breathed billions of stars into existence. You and I cannot stand in the direct power of just one star any more than we can stand in the Lord's direct, manifested presence, as we are.

After a couple of years of walking in this attached, devoted relationship with the Lord, I felt Him pull away. I didn't understand what was happening, but in the coming months I would. As I've told you, tragedies began to occur in my life and the lives of my family members. So many of them happened over the course of several years that we often described our lives as "living in a war zone." We had, without our knowledge or consent, been enlisted onto the battleship. And it felt like bombs were dropping all around us. As the years went on like this, I grew angry and bitter toward the Lord.

Since He is sovereign, I knew He had the power to stop these things from happening at any and all points along the way. But He didn't.

"Why?" I kept asking the Lord, "Why?" And as I continuously expressed my monumental disappointment, displeasure and objections during the next eighteen years of my life "in the valley," He was unmoved. "This is not okay... just want You to know that! I know You're listening. This life-blight is *not okay*! I'm not going to tell You I know everything's gonna be alright, because I don't. I'm not going to say, 'It's okay, Lord, I understand,' because I don't."

Hope deferred makes the heart sick and my hope was that the devastations would just stop, already. But my heart became sick, anyway, as my hope for the metaphorical "bombs" to stop dropping, continued to be deferred.

Why have so many of us had to endure so much? I'm sure you've had to ask yourself this at some point in your life. It just doesn't make sense. Unless......you look at our reality in the context of the Bible and what it says about the end of time. As I said in the previous chapter, Jesus is about to come and the church is about to be raptured, just as it explains in 1 Thessalonians, Chapter 4.

"Brothers and sisters, we do not want you to be uninformed about those who sleep in death, so that you do not grieve like the rest of mankind, who have no hope. [14] For we believe that Jesus died and rose again, and so we believe that God will bring with Jesus those who have fallen asleep in Him. [15] According to the Lord's word, we tell you that we who are still alive, who are left until the coming of the Lord, will certainly not precede those who have fallen asleep.[16] For the Lord himself will come down from heaven, with a loud command, with the voice of the archangel and with the trumpet call of God, and the dead in Christ will rise first. [17] After that, we who are still alive and are left will be caught up together with them in the clouds to meet the Lord in the air. And so we will be with the Lord forever."
1 Thessalonians 4: 13-17

"However, no one knows the day or hour when these things will happen, not even the angels in heaven or the Son himself. Only the Father knows. [33] And since you don't know when that time will come, be on guard! Stay alert!
[34] "The coming of the Son of Man can be illustrated by the story of a man going on a long trip. When he left home, he gave each of his slaves instructions about the work they were to do, and he told the gatekeeper to watch for his return. [35] You, too, must keep watch! For you don't know when the master of the household will return—in the evening, at midnight, before dawn, or at daybreak. [36] Don't let him find you sleeping when he arrives without warning. [37] I say to you what I say to everyone: Watch for him!"
Mark 13:32-37

"I will hear what God the LORD will speak, for He will speak peace to His people and to His saints; but let them not turn back to folly."
Psalm 85:8

"I will revive the spirit of the humble, and the heart of the contrite ones."
Isaiah 57:15 (NKJV)

Give Careful Thought:
Is it possible that my pleasures, hopes and dreams, have been stalled or even withheld by You because You are trying to save me from being too attached to this world? Lord, are You trying to get me to lift my eyes off the things of (even the best I can hope for here in) this world, and get me to look up for Your coming? Are You trying to get me to wake up and stay awake, so that I will be diligently watching for You?

Prayer:
Lord Jesus, please come into my heart and cause me to burn with love for You as my highest priority. Don't let me falter in indifference, but rather help me to place my hope entirely in You. Help me to be watchful, setting my priorities right as I look up and wait for Your return. Amen.

28

Return to
Your First Love

Revelation 2: 3-5

*"You have persevered and have endured hardships for my
name, and have not grown weary. Yet I hold this against you: You
have forsaken your First Love. Remember the height from which
you have fallen! Repent and do the things you did at first. If you
do not repent, I will come to you and remove your lampstand from
its place."*

Jesus warned about this "disease" of turning away from our
First Love, and especially about remaining in that state. In the
verses above from Revelation Chapter 2, He gave a serious
warning to the church in Ephesus (v. 5b).

Just the way these scriptures are written tells us a lot – the
people of the church in Ephesus were acting alright. They were
holding up under immense persecution, but they suffered from a
serious heart condition and, even though it was invisible to the
human eye, Jesus was perfectly aware of it. It was unseen…not
outwardly visible by their behavior…and yet it was there: the
disease of the loss of luster and passion for God in their hearts.

This most likely happened because, during the time of the Apostle John's captivity on The Isle of Patmos, when he was given the vision that, in turn, became the book of Revelation, the Church was under intense pressure in the world. The Ephesians had been experiencing persecution that was ubiquitous. They knew that God was sovereign, and therefore they believed that He should have stopped some of the hardships; He should've rescued them from at least some of it; maybe the worst of it or maybe the last part of it. But He didn't. And now, probably after years of wondering why the Lord didn't intervene and stop the abuse and mistreatment coming upon them from the world; they'd grown dispassionate. The constant pressure of chronic persecution had resulted in a loss of love for Him. In Revelation 2: 3-4, Jesus strictly warns them not to stay in that heart-condition and He calls them back to their First Love….Jesus Himself.

People are hurting. And as the culture increasingly embraces the antichrist, the idea of turning to Jesus is becoming less and less attractive to many. But don't let the fleeting "culture of the day" influence you away from the Lover of your soul. And, if you're a Christian whose love for Jesus has lost its luster; don't settle for this condition in your life. You know it's not what's best for you.

Jesus knew the world would get darker and people, in general, would get more wicked toward the end of the Church Age. That's now and that's exactly what's happening. Now more than ever before, we must heed Jesus' directions about this heart condition.

Either ignite your love for Jesus for the first time, or re-ignite it once and for all. If you've been a Christian for a while, return to the things you did at first. Lean into Him. Spend time everyday meditating on His word (Joshua 1:8), praising and praying. Time spent reading the Word of God will only benefit you; it will never harm you. The Bible says that by reading it, your mind will be washed and renewed, your spirit will be stirred up, and your soul will be healed and given peace.

Give Careful Thought:

Is "Jesus just alright with me" the philosophy you hold toward Him? Have you let your love for Jesus grow cold to the point that you've turned away, even slightly, from your First Love? If your attitude toward the King of the Universe smacks of indifference, recognize now that this is nowhere near being good enough for Him. He deserves your time and attention. He deserves the place of highest reverence and honor in your heart.

Try praying this prayer:
Lord Jesus, forgive me for letting my love for You, my First Love, cool off. Forgive me for allowing other priorities to distract me from You. No matter what has happened, Lord, please help revive my love for You, once again.

29

Rock Steady

--

Hold on Tight

Haggai 2: 6-7

"This is what the LORD Almighty says: 'In a little while I will shake the heavens and the earth, the sea and dry land. I will shake all nations, and the Desired of All Nations (that is, Jesus Christ) will come...and I will fill this house with glory.'"

Zechariah 3:8

"Listen, O high priest Joshua and your associates seated among you who are symbolic of things to come....I am going to bring my Servant, The Branch."

The parable of the persistent widow can be found in Luke, Chapter 18. Jesus was telling it to His disciples to make the point that they should always pray and never give up. The parable is about a godless judge who was approached again and again by a widow who wanted justice. She was unrelenting about it and finally the judge got sick of her and granted her request, even though he didn't care about her, about God, or about justice. He just wanted to get her out of his hair, once and for all.

Jesus points out that if that godless judge will grant justice, God surely will all the more, for He is morally just and cares about those who are His.

"And the Lord said, 'Listen to what the unjust judge says. [7] And will not God bring about justice for his chosen ones, who cry out to him day and night? Will he keep putting them off? [8] I tell you, he will see that they get justice, and quickly. However, when the Son of Man comes, will He find faith on the earth?'"
Luke 18:6-8

"I am coming soon. Hold on to what you have, so that no one will take your crown. [12] The one who is victorious I will make a pillar in the temple of my God. Never again will they leave it."
Revelation 3:11-12

Don't give up. If you can't do anything else, just stand.

"Therefore put on the full armor of God, so that when the day of evil comes, you may be able to stand your ground, and after you have done everything, to stand. [14] Stand firm then...."
Ephesians 6:13-14

"Because of the increase of wickedness, the love of most will grow cold, but the one who stands firm to the end will be saved."
Matthew 24: 12-13

Give Careful Thought:
Consider praying this prayer for yourself and your family members and loved ones:

Lord Jesus, please hold onto us and don't let us go. Please hear our prayers, restore our hope in You, renew our minds, reignite our hearts to burn for You, and solidify our faith in You, *no matter what happens*. Amen.

The Attributes of God

"I am the Alpha and the Omega," says the Lord God, "Who Is, and Who Was, and Who Is To Come, the Almighty."
Revelation 1:8

God is Supreme

Highest in rank, power, authority; superior, highest in degree; utmost.

Genesis 14:19
"and he blessed Abram, saying,
'Blessed be Abram by God Most High,
　　Creator of heaven and earth.'"

Job 11:7-9
"Can you fathom the mysteries of God?
　　Can you probe the limits of the Almighty?
8 They are higher than the heavens above—what can you do?
　　They are deeper than the depths below—what can you know?

⁹ Their measure is longer than the earth
and wider than the sea."

Isaiah 44:6-8
"This is what the LORD says—
Israel's King and Redeemer, the LORD Almighty:
I am the first and I am the last;
apart from me there is no God.
⁷ Who then is like me? Let him proclaim it.
Let him declare and lay out before me
what has happened since I established my ancient people,
and what is yet to come—
yes, let them foretell what will come.
⁸ Do not tremble, do not be afraid.
Did I not proclaim this and foretell it long ago?
You are my witnesses. Is there any God besides me?
No, there is no other Rock; I know not one."

Hebrews 1:4, 6
4) " So he became as much superior to the angels as the name he
has inherited is superior to theirs."

6) "And again, when God brings his firstborn into the world, he
says,
"Let all God's angels worship him."

Deuteronomy 10:14-17
"To the LORD your God belong the heavens, even the highest
heavens, the earth and everything in it. ¹⁵ Yet the LORD set his
affection on your ancestors and loved them, and he chose
you, their descendants, above all the nations—as it is
today. ¹⁶ Circumcise your hearts, therefore, and do not be stiff-

necked any longer. [17] For the LORD your God is God of gods and Lord of lords, the great God, mighty and awesome, who shows no partiality and accepts no bribes."

Psalm 95:3-7

"For the LORD is the great God,
    the great King above all gods.
[4] In his hand are the depths of the earth,
    and the mountain peaks belong to him.
[5] The sea is his, for he made it,
    and his hands formed the dry land.
[6] Come, let us bow down in worship,
    let us kneel before the LORD our Maker;
[7] for he is our God
    and we are the people of his pasture,
    the flock under his care.
Today, if only you would hear his voice,"

Acts 17:24-28

[24] "The God who made the world and everything in it is the Lord of heaven and earth and does not live in temples built by human hands. [25] And he is not served by human hands, as if he needed anything. Rather, he himself gives everyone life and breath and everything else. [26] From one man he made all the nations, that they should inhabit the whole earth; and he marked out their appointed times in history and the boundaries of their lands. [27] God did this so that they would seek him and perhaps reach out for him and find him, though he is not far from any one of us. [28] 'For in him we live and move and have our being. As some of your own poets have said, 'We are his offspring.'"

Jude 24-25
Doxology
24 To him who is able to keep you from stumbling and to present you before his glorious presence without fault and with great joy— 25 to the only God our Savior be glory, majesty, power and authority, through Jesus Christ our Lord, before all ages, now and forevermore! Amen.

Nehemiah 9:6
6 You alone are the LORD. You made the heavens, even the highest heavens, and all their starry host, the earth and all that is on it, the seas and all that is in them. You give life to everything, and the multitudes of heaven worship you.

Psalm 135:5
"I know that the LORD is great,
that our Lord is greater than all gods."

Colossians 1:15-18
The Supremacy of the Son of God
15 The Son is the image of the invisible God, the firstborn over all creation. 16 For in him all things were created: things in heaven and on earth, visible and invisible, whether thrones or powers or rulers or authorities; all things have been created through him and for him.17 He is before all things, and in him all things hold together. 18 And he is the head of the body, the church; he is the beginning and the firstborn from among the dead, so that in everything he might have the supremacy.

Revelation 4:8

[8] Each of the four living creatures had six wings and was covered with eyes all around, even under its wings. Day and night they never stop saying:

> "'Holy, holy, holy
> is the Lord God Almighty,'[a]
> who was, and is, and is to come."

<u>God is Sovereign</u>

Holding the position of ruler, royal, reigning; independent of all others; above or superior to all others; controls everything, can do anything.

1 Samuel 2:6-8
"The LORD brings death and makes alive;
   he brings down to the grave and raises up.
[7] The LORD sends poverty and wealth;
   he humbles and he exalts.
[8] He raises the poor from the dust
   and lifts the needy from the ash heap;
he seats them with princes
   and has them inherit a throne of honor.
"For the foundations of the earth are the LORD's;
   on them he has set the world.

Job 42:2
"I know that you can do all things;
   no purpose of yours can be thwarted."

Psalm 93
"The LORD reigns, he is robed in majesty;
   the LORD is robed in majesty and armed with strength;
   indeed, the world is established, firm and secure.
[2] Your throne was established long ago;
   you are from all eternity.
[3] The seas have lifted up, LORD,
   the seas have lifted up their voice;

the seas have lifted up their pounding waves.
4 Mightier than the thunder of the great waters,
   mightier than the breakers of the sea—
   the LORD on high is mighty.
5 Your statutes, LORD, stand firm;
   holiness adorns your house
   for endless days.

Isaiah 46:9-10

"Remember the former things, those of long ago;
   I am God, and there is no other;
   I am God, and there is none like me.
10 I make known the end from the beginning,
   from ancient times, what is still to come.
I say, 'My purpose will stand,
   and I will do all that I please.'"

1 Chronicles 29:10-13
David's Prayer
10 David praised the LORD in the presence of the whole assembly,
saying,
"Praise be to you, LORD,
   the God of our father Israel,
   from everlasting to everlasting.
11 Yours, LORD, is the greatness and the power
   and the glory and the majesty and the splendor,
   for everything in heaven and earth is yours.
Yours, LORD, is the kingdom;
   you are exalted as head over all.
12 Wealth and honor come from you;
   you are the ruler of all things.
In your hands are strength and power

to exalt and give strength to all.
13 Now, our God, we give you thanks,
and praise your glorious name.

Psalm 33:10-11

"The LORD foils the plans of the nations;
he thwarts the purposes of the peoples.
11 But the plans of the LORD stand firm forever,
the purposes of his heart through all generations."

Psalm 135:6-7

"The LORD does whatever pleases him,
in the heavens and on the earth,
in the seas and all their depths.
7 He makes clouds rise from the ends of the earth;
he sends lightning with the rain
and brings out the wind from his storehouses.

Matthew 10:29-30

"Are not two sparrows sold for a penny? Yet not one of them will
fall to the ground outside your Father's care. 30 And even the very
hairs of your head are all numbered."

2 Chronicles 20:6

6 and said:
"LORD, the God of our ancestors, are you not the God who is in
heaven? You rule over all the kingdoms of the nations. Power and
might are in your hand, and no one can withstand you.

Psalm 47:2-3, 7-8

4) "For the LORD Most High is awesome,
   the great King over all the earth.
3) He subdued nations under us,
   peoples under our feet."

7) "For God is the King of all the earth;
   sing to him a psalm of praise.
8) God reigns over the nations;
   God is seated on his holy throne."

Isaiah 40:10

"See, the Sovereign LORD comes with power,
   and he rules with a mighty arm.
See, his reward is with him,
   and his recompense accompanies him."

Romans 8:28

[28] And we know that in all things God works for the good of those who love him, who[a] have been called according to his purpose.

God is Omnipotent

All powerful; having unlimited power or authority; almighty.

2 Chronicles 32:7-8
[7] "Be strong and courageous. Do not be afraid or discouraged because of the king of Assyria and the vast army with him, for there is a greater power with us than with him. [8] With him is only the arm of flesh, but with us is the LORD our God to help us and to fight our battles." And the people gained confidence from what Hezekiah the king of Judah said.

Psalm 147:5
"Great is our Lord and mighty in power;
    his understanding has no limit."

Habakkuk 3:4
"His splendor was like the sunrise;
    rays flashed from his hand,
    where his power was hidden."

Ephesians 3:20
"Now to him who is able to do immeasurably more than all we ask or imagine, according to his power that is at work within us..."

Psalm 62:11

"One thing God has spoken,
  two things I have heard:
"Power belongs to you, God,"

Isaiah 40:28-31

"Do you not know?
  Have you not heard?
The LORD is the everlasting God,
  the Creator of the ends of the earth.
He will not grow tired or weary,
  and his understanding no one can fathom.
²⁹ He gives strength to the weary
  and increases the power of the weak.
³⁰ Even youths grow tired and weary,
  and young men stumble and fall;
³¹ but those who hope in the LORD
  will renew their strength.
They will soar on wings like eagles;
  they will run and not grow weary,
  they will walk and not be faint."

Matthew 19:26

"Jesus looked at them and said, "With man this is impossible, but with God all things are possible.""

Colossians 1:10-12

"…so that you may live a life worthy of the Lord and please him in every way: bearing fruit in every good work, growing in the knowledge of God, ¹¹ being strengthened with all power according to his glorious might so that you may have great endurance and patience, ¹² and giving joyful thanks to the

Father, who has qualified you[a] to share in the inheritance of his holy people in the kingdom of light.

Psalm 89:8-13

"Who is like you, LORD God Almighty?
   You, LORD, are mighty, and your faithfulness surrounds you.
9 You rule over the surging sea;
   when its waves mount up, you still them.
10 You crushed Rahab like one of the slain;
   with your strong arm you scattered your enemies.
11 The heavens are yours, and yours also the earth;
   you founded the world and all that is in it.
12 You created the north and the south;
   Tabor and Hermon sing for joy at your name.
13 Your arm is endowed with power;
   your hand is strong, your right hand exalted."

Jeremiah 32:17

"Ah, Sovereign LORD, you have made the heavens and the earth by your great power and outstretched arm. Nothing is too hard for you."

Ephesians 1:19-20

"…and his incomparably great power for us who believe. That powe ris the same as the mighty strength 20 he exerted when he raised Christ from the dead and seated him at his right hand in the heavenly realms…"

Hebrews 1:3

"The Son is the radiance of God's glory and the exact representation of his being, sustaining all things by his powerful word. After he had provided purification for sins, he sat down at the right hand of the Majesty in heaven."

God is Omniscient

Having infinite knowledge; knowing all things.

Psalm 44:21
"would not God have discovered it,
   since he knows the secrets of the heart?"

Psalm 147:5
"Great is our Lord and mighty in power;
   his understanding has no limit."

Matthew 6:8
"Do not be like them, for your Father knows what you
need before you ask him."

Romans 11:33-34
Doxology
[33] Oh, the depth of the riches of the wisdom and knowledge of
God!
   How unsearchable his judgments,
   and his paths beyond tracing out!
[34] "Who has known the mind of the Lord?
   Or who has been his counselor?"

Psalm 139:1-6
"You have searched me, LORD,
   and you know me.
[2] You know when I sit and when I rise;
   you perceive my thoughts from afar.

³ You discern my going out and my lying down;
 you are familiar with all my ways.
⁴ Before a word is on my tongue
 you, LORD, know it completely.
⁵ You hem me in behind and before,
 and you lay your hand upon me.
⁶ Such knowledge is too wonderful for me,
 too lofty for me to attain."

Isaiah 65:24
"Before they call I will answer;
 while they are still speaking I will hear."

Matthew 10:30
"And even the very hairs of your head are all numbered."

Colossians 2:3
"…in whom are hidden all the treasures of wisdom and
knowledge."

Psalm 142:3
 "When my spirit grows faint within me,
 it is you who watch over my way.
In the path where I walk
 people have hidden a snare for me."

Daniel 2:22
"He reveals deep and hidden things;
 he knows what lies in darkness,
 and light dwells with him."

John 6:64

"'Yet there are some of you who do not believe." For Jesus had known from the beginning which of them did not believe and who would betray him."

Hebrews 4:13

"Nothing in all creation is hidden from God's sight. Everything is uncovered and laid bare before the eyes of him to whom we must give account."

God is Omnipresent

Present at all places at all times.

1 Kings 8:27
"But will God really dwell on earth? The heavens, even the highest heaven, cannot contain you. How much less this temple I have built!"

Psalm 139:5-12
"You hem me in behind and before,
   and you lay your hand upon me.
[6] Such knowledge is too wonderful for me,
   too lofty for me to attain.
[7] Where can I go from your Spirit?
   Where can I flee from your presence?
[8] If I go up to the heavens, you are there;
   if I make my bed in the depths, you are there.
[9] If I rise on the wings of the dawn,
   if I settle on the far side of the sea,
[10] even there your hand will guide me,
   your right hand will hold me fast.
[11] If I say, "Surely the darkness will hide me
   and the light become night around me,"
[12] even the darkness will not be dark to you;
   the night will shine like the day,
   for darkness is as light to you."

Matthew 28:20

"…and teaching them to obey everything I have commanded you. And surely I am with you always, to the very end of the age."

Colossians 1:17

"He is before all things, and in him all things hold together."

Psalm 31:20

"In the shelter of your presence you hide them
    from all human intrigues;
you keep them safe in your dwelling
    from accusing tongues."

Isaiah 66:1

"Heaven is my throne,
    and the earth is my footstool.
Where is the house you will build for me?
    Where will my resting place be?"

Acts 17:27-28

"God did this so that they would seek him and perhaps reach out for him and find him, though he is not far from any one of us. [28] 'For in him we live and move and have our being.' As some of your own poets have said, 'We are his offspring.'"

2 Timothy 4:16-18

"At my first defense, no one came to my support, but everyone deserted me. May it not be held against them. [17] But the Lord stood at my side and gave me strength, so that through me the message might be fully proclaimed and all the Gentiles might hear it. And I was delivered from the lion's mouth. [18] The Lord will rescue me from every evil attack and will bring me safely to his heavenly kingdom. To him be glory for ever and ever. Amen."

Psalm 46:1-7

"God is our refuge and strength,
an ever-present help in trouble.
² Therefore we will not fear, though the earth give way
and the mountains fall into the heart of the sea,
³ though its waters roar and foam
and the mountains quake with their surging.[c]
⁴ There is a river whose streams make glad the city of God,
the holy place where the Most High dwells.
⁵ God is within her, she will not fall;
God will help her at break of day.
⁶ Nations are in uproar, kingdoms fall;
he lifts his voice, the earth melts.
⁷ The LORD Almighty is with us;
the God of Jacob is our fortress."

Jeremiah 23:24

"Who can hide in secret places
so that I cannot see them?"
declares the LORD.
"Do not I fill heaven and earth?"
declares the LORD."

Romans 8:35, 38-39

35) "Who shall separate us from the love of Christ? Shall trouble or hardship or persecution or famine or nakedness or danger or sword?"

38) "For I am convinced that neither death nor life, neither angels nor demons, neither the present nor the future, nor any powers, ³⁹ neither height nor depth, nor anything else in all

creation, will be able to separate us from the love of God that is in Christ Jesus our Lord."

Hebrews 13:5

"Keep your lives free from the love of money and be content with what you have, because God has said,
"Never will I leave you;
    never will I forsake you."

God is Immutable

Never changing or varying; unchangeable.

Numbers 23:19
"God is not human, that he should lie,
   not a human being, that he should change his mind.
Does he speak and then not act?
   Does he promise and not fulfill?"

Psalm 100:5
"For the LORD is good and his love endures forever;
   his faithfulness continues through all generations."

Isaiah 40:6-8
"A voice says, "Cry out."
   And I said, "What shall I cry?"
"All people are like grass,
   and all their faithfulness is like the flowers of the field.
[7] The grass withers and the flowers fall,
   because the breath of the LORD blows on them.
   Surely the people are grass.
[8] The grass withers and the flowers fall,
   but the word of our God endures forever."

Hebrews 6:17-19a
"Because God wanted to make the unchanging nature of his
purpose very clear to the heirs of what was promised, he
confirmed it with an oath. [18] God did this so that, by two
unchangeable things in which it is impossible for God to lie, we
who have fled to take hold of the hope set before us may be

greatly encouraged. [19] We have this hope as an anchor for the soul, firm and secure."

1 Samuel 15:29
"He who is the Glory of Israel does not lie or change his mind; for he is not a human being, that he should change his mind."

Psalm 102:25-27
"In the beginning you laid the foundations of the earth,
   and the heavens are the work of your hands.
[26] They will perish, but you remain;
   they will all wear out like a garment.
Like clothing you will change them
   and they will be discarded.
[27] But you remain the same,
   and your years will never end."

Isaiah 51:6
"Lift up your eyes to the heavens,
   look at the earth beneath;
the heavens will vanish like smoke,
   the earth will wear out like a garment
   and its inhabitants die like flies.
But my salvation will last forever,
   my righteousness will never fail."

Hebrews 13:8
" Jesus Christ is the same yesterday and today and forever."

Psalm 33:11
"But the plans of the LORD stand firm forever,
   the purposes of his heart through all generations."

Psalm 119:89, 152

89) "Your word, LORD, is eternal;
    it stands firm in the heavens."

152) "Long ago I learned from your statutes
    that you established them to last forever."

Malachi 3:6a

"I the LORD do not change. So you, the descendants of Jacob, are not destroyed."

James 1:17

"Every good and perfect gift is from above, coming down from the Father of the heavenly lights, who does not change like shifting shadows."

God is Faithful

Constant, loyal, reliable, steadfast, unwavering, devoted, true, dependable.

Deuteronomy 7:9
" Know therefore that the LORD your God is God; he is the faithful God, keeping his covenant of love to a thousand generations of those who love him and keep his commandments."

Psalm 119:90
"Your faithfulness continues through all generations;
    you established the earth, and it endures."

Lamentations 3:21-24
"Yet this I call to mind
    and therefore I have hope:
22 Because of the LORD's great love we are not consumed,
    for his compassions never fail.
23 They are new every morning;
    great is your faithfulness.
24 I say to myself, "The LORD is my portion;
    therefore I will wait for him."

2 Timothy 2:13
"…if we are faithless,
    he remains faithful,
        for he cannot disown himself."

Psalm 33:4

"For the word of the LORD is right and true;
　he is faithful in all he does."

Psalm 145:13

"Your kingdom is an everlasting kingdom,
　and your dominion endures through all generations.
The LORD is trustworthy in all he promises
　and faithful in all he does."

1 Corinthians 10:13

"No temptation has overtaken you except what is common to
mankind. And God is faithful; he will not let you be
tempted beyond what you can bear. But when you are tempted, he
will also provide a way out so that you can endure it."

1 John 1:9

" If we confess our sins, he is faithful and just and will forgive us
our sins and purify us from all unrighteousness."

Psalm 89:8

"Who is like you, LORD God Almighty?
　You, LORD, are mighty, and your faithfulness surrounds you."

Psalm 146:5-8

"Blessed are those whose help is the God of Jacob,
　whose hope is in the LORD their God.
⁶ He is the Maker of heaven and earth,
　the sea, and everything in them—
　he remains faithful forever.
⁷ He upholds the cause of the oppressed
　and gives food to the hungry.

The LORD sets prisoners free,

8 the LORD gives sight to the blind,
the LORD lifts up those who are bowed down,
the LORD loves the righteous."

2 Timothy 1:12

"That is why I am suffering as I am. Yet this is no cause for shame, because I know whom I have believed, and am convinced that he is able to guard what I have entrusted to him until that day."

Revelation 19:11
The Heavenly Warrior Defeats the Beast

" I saw heaven standing open and there before me was a white horse, whose rider is called Faithful and True. With justice he judges and wages war."

Psalm 103: 13-17

13 As a father has compassion on his children,
so the LORD has compassion on those who fear him;
14 for he knows how we are formed,
he remembers that we are dust.
15 The life of mortals is like grass,
they flourish like a flower of the field;
16 the wind blows over it and it is gone,
and its place remembers it no more.
17 But from everlasting to everlasting
the LORD's love is with those who fear him,
and his righteousness with their children's children—

God is Holy

Spiritually perfect or pure; sinless; deserving awe, reverence, adoration.

Exodus 15:11

"Who among the gods
    is like you, LORD?
Who is like you—
    majestic in holiness,
awesome in glory,
    working wonders?"

Psalm 99

"The LORD reigns,
    let the nations tremble;
he sits enthroned between the cherubim,
    let the earth shake.
2 Great is the LORD in Zion;
    he is exalted over all the nations.
3 Let them praise your great and awesome name—
    he is holy.
4 The King is mighty, he loves justice—
    you have established equity;
in Jacob you have done
    what is just and right.
5 Exalt the LORD our God
    and worship at his footstool;
    he is holy.

⁶ Moses and Aaron were among his priests,
   Samuel was among those who called on his name;
they called on the LORD
   and he answered them.
⁷ He spoke to them from the pillar of cloud;
   they kept his statutes and the decrees he gave them.
⁸ LORD our God,
   you answered them;
you were to Israel a forgiving God,
   though you punished their misdeeds.
⁹ Exalt the LORD our God
   and worship at his holy mountain,
   for the LORD our God is holy."

Isaiah 57:15-16

"For this is what the high and exalted One says—
   he who lives forever, whose name is holy:
"I live in a high and holy place,
   but also with the one who is contrite and lowly in spirit,
to revive the spirit of the lowly
   and to revive the heart of the contrite.
¹⁶ I will not accuse them forever,
   nor will I always be angry,
for then they would faint away because of me—
   the very people I have created."

1 Peter 1:15-16

"But just as he who called you is holy, so be holy in all you
do; ¹⁶ for it is written: "Be holy, because I am holy.""

1 Samuel 2:2

"There is no one holy like the LORD;
   there is no one besides you;
   there is no Rock like our God."

Psalm 111:9

"He provided redemption for his people;
   he ordained his covenant forever—
   holy and awesome is his name."

Luke 1:49

"…for the Mighty One has done great things for me—
   holy is His name."

Revelation 4:8

"Each of the four living creatures had six wings and was covered with eyes all around, even under its wings. Day and night they never stop saying:
            "'Holy, holy, holy
         is the Lord God Almighty,'
      who was, and is, and is to come."

Psalm 77:13

"Your ways, God, are holy.
   What god is as great as our God?"

Isaiah 5:16

"But the LORD Almighty will be exalted by his justice,
   and the holy God will be proved holy by his righteous acts."

Acts 3:13-15

"The God of Abraham, Isaac and Jacob, the God of our fathers, has glorified his servant Jesus. You handed him over to be killed, and you disowned him before Pilate, though he had decided to let him go. [14] You disowned the Holy and Righteous One and asked that a murderer be released to you. [15] You killed the author of life, but God raised him from the dead. We are witnesses of this."

Revelation 15:4

"Who will not fear you, Lord,
    and bring glory to your name?
For you alone are holy.
All nations will come
    and worship before you,
for your righteous acts have been revealed."

<u>God is Just</u>

Right or fair; impartial, upright, lawful, correct, true; righteous.

Deuteronomy 32:4

"He is the Rock, his works are perfect,
   and all his ways are just.
A faithful God who does no wrong,
   upright and just is he."

Psalm 89:14-16

"Righteousness and justice are the foundation of your throne;
   love and faithfulness go before you.
¹⁵ Blessed are those who have learned to acclaim you,
   who walk in the light of your presence, LORD.
¹⁶ They rejoice in your name all day long;
   they celebrate your righteousness."

Isaiah 30:18

"Yet the LORD longs to be gracious to you;
   therefore he will rise up to show you compassion.
For the LORD is a God of justice.
   Blessed are all who wait for him!"

Romans 3:25-26

"God presented Christ as a sacrifice of atonement, through the shedding of his blood—to be received by faith. He did this to demonstrate his righteousness, because in his forbearance he had left the sins committed beforehand unpunished— ²⁶ he did it to demonstrate his righteousness at the present time, so as to be just and the one who justifies those who have faith in Jesus."

2 Chronicles 19:7

"Now let the fear of the LORD be on you. Judge carefully, for with the LORD our God there is no injustice or partiality or bribery."

Psalm 119:137-138

"You are righteous, LORD,
   and your laws are right.
138 The statutes you have laid down are righteous;
   they are fully trustworthy."

Zephaniah 3:5

"The LORD within her is righteous;
   he does no wrong.
Morning by morning he dispenses his justice,
   and every new day he does not fail,
   yet the unrighteous know no shame."

2 Thessalonians 1:5-7

"All this is evidence that God's judgment is right, and as a result you will be counted worthy of the kingdom of God, for which you are suffering. 6 God is just: He will pay back trouble to those who trouble you 7 and give relief to you who are troubled, and to us as well. This will happen when the Lord Jesus is revealed from heaven in blazing fire with his powerful angels."

Psalm 9:7-10

"The LORD reigns forever;
   he has established his throne for judgment.
8 He rules the world in righteousness
   and judges the peoples with equity.
9 The LORD is a refuge for the oppressed,
   a stronghold in times of trouble.

[10] Those who know your name trust in you,
    for you, LORD, have never forsaken those who seek you."

Psalm 103:6
"The LORD works righteousness and justice
for all the oppressed."

Psalm 145:17
"The LORD is righteous in all his ways
    and faithful in all he does."

John 5:30
"By myself I can do nothing; I judge only as I hear, and my
judgment is just, for I seek not to please myself but him who sent
me."

Revelation 15:3-4
"and sang the song of God's servant Moses and of the Lamb:
"Great and marvelous are your deeds,
    Lord God Almighty.
Just and true are your ways,
    King of the nations.
[4] Who will not fear you, Lord,
    and bring glory to your name?
For you alone are holy.
All nations will come
    and worship before you,
for your righteous acts have been revealed."

God is Wise

From the root word *to know* or *to see*, but wisdom goes past knowledge to understanding and action; having keen perception, discernment; power of judging rightly; always making right choices.

1 Chronicles 28:9
"And you, my son Solomon, acknowledge the God of your father, and serve him with wholehearted devotion and with a willing mind, for the LORD searches every heart and understands every desire and every thought. If you seek him, he will be found by you; but if you forsake him, he will reject you forever."

Proverbs 2:6
"For the LORD gives wisdom;
    from his mouth come knowledge and understanding."

Isaiah 55:8-9
"For my thoughts are not your thoughts,
    neither are your ways my ways,"
declares the LORD.
⁹ "As the heavens are higher than the earth,
    so are my ways higher than your ways
    and my thoughts than your thoughts."

Romans 16:27
"to the only wise God be glory forever through Jesus Christ! Amen."

Psalm 92:5

"How great are your works, LORD,
   how profound your thoughts!"

Proverbs 3:19-20

"By wisdom the LORD laid the earth's foundations,
   by understanding he set the heavens in place;
[20] by his knowledge the watery depths were divided,
   and the clouds let drop the dew."

Daniel 2:20-22

"…and said:

"Praise be to the name of God for ever and ever;
   wisdom and power are his.
[21] He changes times and seasons;
   he deposes kings and raises up others.
He gives wisdom to the wise
   and knowledge to the discerning.
[22] He reveals deep and hidden things;
   he knows what lies in darkness,
   and light dwells with him."

Colossians 2:2-3

" My goal is that they may be encouraged in heart and united in love, so that they may have the full riches of complete understanding, in order that they may know the mystery of God, namely, Christ, [3] in whom are hidden all the treasures of wisdom and knowledge."

Psalm 147:5

"Great is our Lord and mighty in power;
   his understanding has no limit."

Isaiah 28:29

"All this also comes from the LORD Almighty,
   whose plan is wonderful,
   whose wisdom is magnificent."

Romans 11:33-34
Doxology

  "Oh, the depth of the riches of the wisdom and knowledge of
God!
   How unsearchable his judgments,
   and his paths beyond tracing out!
[34] "Who has known the mind of the Lord?
   Or who has been his counselor?"

James 3:17

" But the wisdom that comes from heaven is first of all pure; then
peace-loving, considerate, submissive, full of mercy and good
fruit, impartial and sincere."

<u>God is Eternal</u>

Without beginning or end; existing through all time; everlasting.

Exodus 3:14-15
"God said to Moses, "I AM WHO I AM. This is what you are to say to the Israelites: 'I AM has sent me to you.'"
15 God also said to Moses, "Say to the Israelites, 'The LORD,[b] the God of your fathers—the God of Abraham, the God of Isaac and the God of Jacob—has sent me to you.'
"This is my name forever,
    the name you shall call me
    from generation to generation."

John 8:58
"Very truly I tell you," Jesus answered, "before Abraham was born, I am!"

Nehemiah 9:5b
"And the Levites—Jeshua, Kadmiel, Bani, Hashabneiah, Sherebiah, Hodiah, Shebaniah and Pethahiah—said: "Stand up and praise the LORD your God, who is from everlasting to everlasting."
"Blessed be your glorious name, and may it be exalted above all blessing and praise."

Psalm 93:2
"Your throne was established long ago;
    you are from all eternity."

Romans 1:20

"For since the creation of the world God's invisible qualities—his eternal power and divine nature—have been clearly seen, being understood from what has been made, so that people are without excuse."

Exodus 15:18

"The LORD reigns
    for ever and ever."

Psalm 45:6

"Your throne, O God, will last for ever and ever;
    a scepter of justice will be the scepter of your kingdom."

Isaiah 26:4

"Trust in the LORD forever,
    for the LORD, the LORD himself, is the Rock eternal."

1 Timothy 1:17

"Now to the King eternal, immortal, invisible, the only God, be honor and glory for ever and ever. Amen."

Deuteronomy 33:27

"The eternal God is your refuge,
    and underneath are the everlasting arms.
He will drive out your enemies before you,
    saying, 'Destroy them!'"

Psalm 90:1-2

A prayer of Moses the man of God.

"Lord, you have been our dwelling place
throughout all generations.
² Before the mountains were born
or you brought forth the whole world,
from everlasting to everlasting you are God."

Jeremiah 31:3

"The LORD appeared to us in the past, saying:
"I have loved you with an everlasting love;
I have drawn you with unfailing kindness."

Revelation 1:8,18

⁸ "I am the Alpha and the Omega," says the Lord God, "who is, and who was, and who is to come, the Almighty."

18) "I am the Living One; I was dead, and now look, I am alive for ever and ever! And I hold the keys of death and Hades."

God is the Creator

The one who brought into existence the universe and all matter and life in it.

Genesis 1:1

"In the beginning God created the heavens and the earth."

Psalm 104

"Praise the LORD, my soul.

LORD my God, you are very great;
   you are clothed with splendor and majesty.
2 The LORD wraps himself in light as with a garment;
   he stretches out the heavens like a tent
3   and lays the beams of his upper chambers on their waters.
He makes the clouds his chariot
   and rides on the wings of the wind.
4 He makes winds his messengers,
   flames of fire his servants.
5 He set the earth on its foundations;
   it can never be moved.
6 You covered it with the watery depths as with a garment;
   the waters stood above the mountains.
7 But at your rebuke the waters fled,
   at the sound of your thunder they took to flight;
8 they flowed over the mountains,
   they went down into the valleys,
   to the place you assigned for them.

⁹ You set a boundary they cannot cross;
   never again will they cover the earth.
¹⁰ He makes springs pour water into the ravines;
   it flows between the mountains.
¹¹ They give water to all the beasts of the field;
   the wild donkeys quench their thirst.
¹² The birds of the sky nest by the waters;
   they sing among the branches.
¹³ He waters the mountains from his upper chambers;
   the land is satisfied by the fruit of his work.
¹⁴ He makes grass grow for the cattle,
   and plants for people to cultivate—
   bringing forth food from the earth:
¹⁵ wine that gladdens human hearts,
   oil to make their faces shine,
   and bread that sustains their hearts.
¹⁶ The trees of the LORD are well watered,
   the cedars of Lebanon that he planted.
¹⁷ There the birds make their nests;
   the stork has its home in the junipers.
¹⁸ The high mountains belong to the wild goats;
   the crags are a refuge for the hyrax.
¹⁹ He made the moon to mark the seasons,
   and the sun knows when to go down.
²⁰ You bring darkness, it becomes night,
   and all the beasts of the forest prowl.
²¹ The lions roar for their prey
   and seek their food from God.
²² The sun rises, and they steal away;
   they return and lie down in their dens.
²³ Then people go out to their work,
   to their labor until evening.

²⁴ How many are your works, LORD!
In wisdom you made them all;
the earth is full of your creatures.
²⁵ There is the sea, vast and spacious,
teeming with creatures beyond number—
living things both large and small.
²⁶ There the ships go to and fro,
and Leviathan, which you formed to frolic there.
²⁷ All creatures look to you
to give them their food at the proper time.
²⁸ When you give it to them,
they gather it up;
when you open your hand,
they are satisfied with good things.
²⁹ When you hide your face,
they are terrified;
when you take away their breath,
they die and return to the dust.
³⁰ When you send your Spirit,
they are created,
and you renew the face of the ground.
³¹ May the glory of the LORD endure forever;
may the LORD rejoice in his works—
³² he who looks at the earth, and it trembles,
who touches the mountains, and they smoke.
³³ I will sing to the LORD all my life;
I will sing praise to my God as long as I live.
³⁴ May my meditation be pleasing to him,
as I rejoice in the LORD.
³⁵ But may sinners vanish from the earth
and the wicked be no more.
Praise the LORD, my soul.
Praise the LORD."

Jeremiah 10:12

"But God made the earth by his power;
  he founded the world by his wisdom
  and stretched out the heavens by his understanding."

Colossians 1:16

"For in him all things were created: things in heaven and on earth,
visible and invisible, whether thrones or powers or rulers or
authorities; all things have been created through him and for him."

Psalm 95:3-7

"For the LORD is the great God,
  the great King above all gods.
4 In his hand are the depths of the earth,
  and the mountain peaks belong to him.
5 The sea is his, for he made it,
  and his hands formed the dry land.
6 Come, let us bow down in worship,
  let us kneel before the LORD our Maker;
7 for he is our God
  and we are the people of his pasture,
  the flock under his care.
Today, if only you would hear his voice…"

Psalm 148:1-6

"Praise the LORD.
Praise the LORD from the heavens;
  praise him in the heights above.
2 Praise him, all his angels;
  praise him, all his heavenly hosts.

[3] Praise him, sun and moon;
   praise him, all you shining stars.
[4] Praise him, you highest heavens
   and you waters above the skies.
[5] Let them praise the name of the LORD,
   for at his command they were created,
[6] and he established them for ever and ever—
   he issued a decree that will never pass away."

John 1:3

"Through him all things were made; without him nothing was made that has been made."

Hebrews 1:2

"…but in these last days he has spoken to us by his Son, whom he appointed heir of all things, and through whom also he made the universe."

Psalm 100:3

"Know that the LORD is God.
   It is he who made us, and we are his;
   we are his people, the sheep of his pasture."

Isaiah 42:5

"This is what God the LORD says—
the Creator of the heavens, who stretches them out,
   who spreads out the earth with all that springs from it,

who gives breath to its people,
and life to those who walk on it…"

Acts 17:24-28

"The God who made the world and everything in it is the Lord of heaven and earth and does not live in temples built by human hands.[25] And he is not served by human hands, as if he needed anything. Rather, he himself gives everyone life and breath and everything else.[26] From one man he made all the nations, that they should inhabit the whole earth; and he marked out their appointed times in history and the boundaries of their lands. [27] God did this so that they would seek him and perhaps reach out for him and find him, though he is not far from any one of us. [28] 'For in him we live and move and have our being.' As some of your own poets have said, 'We are his offspring.'"

Revelation 10:6

"And he swore by him who lives for ever and ever, who created the heavens and all that is in them, the earth and all that is in it, and the sea and all that is in it, and said, "There will be no more delay!"

God is Good

Virtuous, excellent; upright; God is essentially, absolutely and consummately good.

Psalm 25:8
"Good and upright is the LORD;
  therefore he instructs sinners in his ways."

Psalm 119:68
"You are good, and what you do is good;
  teach me your decrees."

Jeremiah 33:11
"the sounds of joy and gladness, the voices of bride and bridegroom, and the voices of those who bring thank offerings to the house of the LORD, saying,
"Give thanks to the LORD Almighty,
  for the LORD is good;
  his love endures forever."
For I will restore the fortunes of the land as they were before,'
says the LORD."

John 10:11
"I am the good shepherd. The good shepherd lays down his life for the sheep."

Psalm 34:8

"Taste and see that the LORD is good;
   blessed is the one who takes refuge in him."

Psalm 136:1

"Give thanks to the LORD, for he is good.
His love endures forever."

Nahum 1:7

"The LORD is good,
   a refuge in times of trouble.
He cares for those who trust in him…"

1 Timothy 4:4

"For everything God created is good, and nothing is to be
rejected if it is received with thanksgiving…"

Psalm 86:5

"You, Lord, are forgiving and good,
   abounding in love to all who call to you.
 You, Lord, are forgiving and good,
   abounding in love to all who call to you."

Psalm 145:9

"The LORD is good to all;
   he has compassion on all he has made."

Mark 10:18

"Why do you call me good?" Jesus answered. "No one is good—except God alone."

2 Peter 1:3-4

"His divine power has given us everything we need for a godly life through our knowledge of him who called us by his own glory and goodness. 4 Through these he has given us his very great and precious promises, so that through them you may participate in the divine nature, having escaped the corruption in the world caused by evil desires."

Psalm 103

Praise the LORD, my soul;
    all my inmost being, praise his holy name.
2 Praise the LORD, my soul,
    and forget not all his benefits—
3 who forgives all your sins
    and heals all your diseases,
4 who redeems your life from the pit
    and crowns you with love and compassion,
5 who satisfies your desires with good things
    so that your youth is renewed like the eagle's.
6 The LORD works righteousness
    and justice for all the oppressed.
7 He made known his ways to Moses,
    his deeds to the people of Israel:
8 The LORD is compassionate and gracious,
    slow to anger, abounding in love.
9 He will not always accuse,

nor will he harbor his anger forever;
¹⁰ he does not treat us as our sins deserve
   or repay us according to our iniquities.
¹¹ For as high as the heavens are above the earth,
   so great is his love for those who fear him;
¹² as far as the east is from the west,
   so far has he removed our transgressions from us.
¹³ As a father has compassion on his children,
   so the LORD has compassion on those who fear him;
¹⁴ for he knows how we are formed,
   he remembers that we are dust.
¹⁵ The life of mortals is like grass,
   they flourish like a flower of the field;
¹⁶ the wind blows over it and it is gone,
   and its place remembers it no more.
¹⁷ But from everlasting to everlasting
   the LORD's love is with those who fear him,
   and his righteousness with their children's children—
¹⁸ with those who keep his covenant
   and remember to obey his precepts.
¹⁹ The LORD has established his throne in heaven,
   and his kingdom rules over all.
²⁰ Praise the LORD, you his angels,
   you mighty ones who do his bidding,
   who obey his word.
²¹ Praise the LORD, all his heavenly hosts,
   you his servants who do his will.
²² Praise the LORD, all his works
   everywhere in his dominion.
Praise the LORD, my soul.

Contract With God

Let this contract between the parties, that being God the Father, His Son Jesus Christ, and the Holy Spirit (aka The Holy Trinity) and _____,

be entered into this _____ day of

_____, _____.

I, _____, do hereby acknowledge and declare my faith in the Holy Trinity; that God the Father is, indeed, my father, that He sent His Son, Jesus Christ, to die for my sins, and to take back all authority in heaven and earth. As it pertains to my life, Jesus is my Lord and Savior. I believe He willingly died on the cross to satisfy the required punishment for my sins. I believe He died, was resurrected and rose again, and now sits at the right hand of God the Father in heaven. I believe He is alive.

Furthermore, I believe the same Holy Spirit that raised Jesus from the dead now lives in me (Romans 8:11). I believe the Holy Bible is the only truthful Word of God, and I believe God cannot lie. Therefore, I will believe what God's Word tells me.

I, _____, do hereby give permission for God to work in my life.

I, _____, do hereby declare that I know that God created me to fulfill a specific purpose (my God-Track), and furthermore, I declare that I intend to fulfill it.

I, _____, choose to make Jesus Christ my First Love, and to hold onto Him with a devotion that cannot be broken. I will wait and watch for Him, and put my hope in Him above all else.

I ask You now, Lord Jesus, to show me my God-Track, and to give me the strength, without any fear, to fulfill my earthly mission, just as You've ordained for it to be. Amen.

Signed,

_____

Name   Date

Other books by

Shelly Skiver include:

"Can You Hear Me Now?"

"Find Your End-Time-God-Track

in Three Simple Steps"

Available on amazon.com

"A Guide to Haggai

Bible Study"

(Answer Key also available)

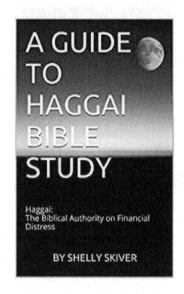

Available on amazon.com

"Solace"

"Finding the Peace God Promises"

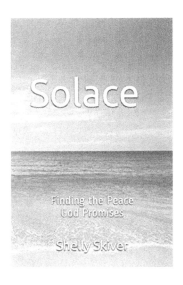

Available on amazon.com

"Divine Synchronicities"

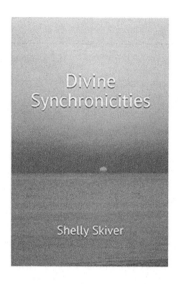

...true-life stories of miraculous happenings some may call "coincidences"

Available on amazon.com

"COUNTDOWN"

....to the Imminent Return of Christ

A prophecy given to Shelly Skiver about the return of Jesus

Available on amazon.com

"Desperate Measures...

One Woman's Journey
From Anger to Peace With God"

Available on amazon.com

Visit our website at:

www.countdown2hisreturn.com

You can contact Shelly Skiver at:

countdown2Hisreturn@gmail.com

To find all of Shelly's books
go to amazon.com and type *Shelly Skiver*
into the search bar.

71117880R00146

Made in the USA
Middletown, DE
30 September 2019